ANJELICA HUSTON

ANJELICA HUSTON

The Lady and the Legacy

MARTHA HARRIS

A 2M Communications Ltd. Production

ST. MARTIN'S PRESS
New York

Photo research by Amanda Rubin

Design by Glen M. Edelstein

Library of Congress Cataloging-in-Publication Data

Harris, Martha.
    Anjelica Huston : the lady and the legacy.

    1. Huston, Anjelica.   2. Motion picture actors and
actresses—United States—Biography.   I. Title.
PN2287.H87H37   1989   791.43′028′0924 [B]   88–29866
ISBN 0-312-02541-6

First Edition

10 9 8 7 6 5 4 3 2 1

ANJELICA HUSTON

CHAPTER 1

*T*HERE are a lot of routes to stardom in Hollywood.

You can sip a soda at the right corner drugstore and be discovered, the way Lana Turner was.

You can try out for a once-in-a-lifetime part and beat out hundreds of other girls, the way Vivian Leigh did.

You can be a gorgeous child star and never go through an awkward age, the way Elizabeth Taylor did.

You can be born into a show-biz family, the way Liza Minelli was. And the way Anjelica Huston was, right?

Wrong.

Although to everyone jolted out of their seats by Anjelica's tour-de-force performance as Maerose Prizzi in *Prizzi's Honor*, it must be the answer to her sudden burst into the limelight. After all, didn't John Huston direct *Prizzi's Honor*? And isn't Anjelica his daughter?

Yes to both questions—but two yeses still don't add up to the right answer.

It could be said that Richard Avedon, the great fashion and portrait photographer, "discovered" Anjelica—because he launched the modeling career that brought her money and fame.

It could be said that Maerose Prizzi, though not the leading role, *was* one of those once-in-a-lifetime parts, making Anjelica an "overnight" star.

It could be said that a childhood peopled with famous actors whose names on movie billboards across America meant money in the bank for their studios set Anjelica up for stardom.

It could be said that when her father put her in a film at age sixteen, he knew Anjelica would someday be a major actress.

All of these things could be said—and each, from one perspective, has some truth. But from another perspective, none of them is totally true. And all of those statements still do not explain the phenomenal success Anjelica Huston scored in her first big role.

To understand how an actress almost no one had heard of suddenly became a household word, one has to go back to the beginning, to Anjelica's birth in July of 1951. Each sequence of her life contributed some essential facet to the scenario that was slowly building. And though other people—her father, her mother, her friend and long-time lover Jack Nicholson—seem to have the dominant roles in all those scenes preceding *Prizzi's Honor*, actually it was Anjelica herself, watching, absorbing, weighing one choice against another, who finally became responsible for her success.

Anjelica discovered herself, through a long and difficult journey.

Anjelica took any role that came along, no matter how small, in the years before she played Maerose.

Anjelica survived that early disastrous film and came back into the ring—scarred but still trying, cowed but not willing to give up.

Anjelica had to learn about family, and what it means, from a father who was never there, and from a mother who died too young.

There were no easy answers for Anjelica. And maybe that's why her Maerose Prizzi is so strong. There weren't any easy answers for Maerose, either.

Prizzi's Honor, based on the novel by Richard Condon, is a simple enough story. The Prizzis are a Mafia family, led by Don Corrado Prizzi. Charley Partanna (Jack Nicholson) is their top hit man. When a job comes up that calls for someone outside the "Family," Irene Walker (Kathleen Turner) is hired. She is a freelance killer, married to a man who runs one of the Prizzis' Las Vegas gambling casinos. Charley, who carries out the Don's orders but doesn't sit in on policy sessions, meets Irene at a "Family" wedding and is immediately smitten. She is married—but it is her husband Charley has been ordered to kill, because he has been stealing from the Family's casinos. Only after Charley has removed Irene's husband, thus clearing the way for him to marry her and getting rid of a thief at one and the same time, does he find out that Irene was in on the theft. Now Charley has another target—his beloved.

And Maerose? Maerose is the Don's granddaughter. When the film opens, she is an outcast because she had a fling with another man while engaged to Charley. The fling meant nothing to her—it was her way of rebelling against the Family. She has always loved Charley and she loves him still. And from the very first moment of their meeting at the wedding reception, Maerose has but one goal. Get Charley back.

"One thing about Maerose is that she's going to be there," Anjelica said. "She's hands-on. She goes about her intention. She's a woman living very much in the present who's not at all pre-occupied with her past. . . . I found her very empathetic . . . a lot of people saw her as a monster-woman. But she's been hurt in the past. She's had some problems and she has to get through it in the way that she gets through it."

This quality is part of Maerose's special appeal. One scene in the movie particularly brings it out. Charley comes to Maerose after he has discovered that Irene Walker has the money her husband stole from the Family's casinos. "Do I ice her? Do I marry her?" he asks Maerose. "The calendar will take care of everything," Maerose says, but there's little question whose hand will be turning the pages.

Nor does Maerose hide her motives from Charley. When he comes to see her for the first time in years, Maerose says, "Let's do it. Right here on the Oriental."

The fact that the man playing Charley happened to be Anjelica's long-time lover only heightened the challenge of her role. Up until *Prizzi's Honor*, Anjelica had been a struggling actress seen often holding onto Nicholson's arm. Emerging from her longtime real-life role as a background extra in other, more celebrated lives, Anjelica made critical jaws drop with "the awesome aplomb" with which she "blew Kathleen Turner off the screen as effectively as Maerose had blown her out of Charley Partanna's life."

And Nicholson ate it up. He saw *Prizzi's Honor* as a "career maker" for Anjelica, adding that she is "flawless" in the role. He had been "silently hoping for Anjelica's success as an actress" and took particular pleasure in the fact that her success began in a picture they worked on together. Nicholson was glad, too, that the success came in a film Anjelica's father directed.

He remarked on the fact that "it was a big deal for her and her father, John Huston, to work successfully together. There was a lot of grit between them on the subject of *A Walk With Love and Death* [the film John put Anjelica in when she was sixteen]. They seemed to have had two separate experiences, equally baffling to both of them. But it was obvious how exhilarated John was by the material, and by how much she has grown as an actress. She responded to that, of course, so it did give the experience a special quality."

Nicholson had wanted to be in a film directed by John Huston for a long time. They had acted together in Roman Polanski's *Chinatown*, but *Prizzi's Honor* was the first time Jack would work with John as actor and director. But at the beginning Jack didn't even understand the story, much less think he could play the slow-witted, love-smitten Charley. Only by that time, Anjelica already had her part. If Nicholson wanted to play opposite her—if he wanted to work with John Huston—he would have to take the plunge. He took it.

The line between art and life is always blurred, and very often artists themselves can't tell where one ends and the other begins. The way *Prizzi's Honor* came together in the first place reads like a story—in this case a fairy tale with the traditional happy ending.

It all began when John Huston found the galleys of Richard Condon's novel in his house at Puerto Vallarta. Condon had sent Huston *Prizzi's Honor* two years before; the two men had known each other for thirty years, and Huston had helped get Condon's first novel, *The Oldest Confession*, made into a movie.

Huston read the galleys, loved the book and its matter-of-fact attitude toward evil, and called John Foreman, a producer with whom he had worked before, to find out if the novel was available for filming.

Was it fate that made John Huston mislay those galleys for two years? If not, then it was pure blind luck. Two years earlier the configuration of people that made *Prizzi's Honor* a brilliant success would have been involved in other projects, would have been in other places in their lives. But they *did* get mislaid—and when Huston read them, everything was ready. His interest in the project lit the first creative spark, a spark that burned brighter and brighter until it made a spotlight for the woman who played Maerose.

Because at the very time Huston called Foreman, Foreman had just finished making *Ice Pirates* with Anjelica in a lead role. No matter that the critics didn't like the movie, and that it didn't do very well at the box office. Foreman saw what Anjelica could do—and when he read *Prizzi's Honor*, he knew immediately she could play Maerose.

Anjelica then set about talking Nicholson into playing the part of Charley. John Huston needed no talking to—he and Foreman had been a director-producer team three times before, on *The Man Who Would Be King, The Mackintosh Man*, and *The Life and Times of Judge Roy Bean*. He loved the idea that these professional killers go about their dirty work as though it is a normal, everyday business. This is how they earn their living—and after they do it, they go home and have a life just like everybody else. That, Huston thought, gave the story its comic value.

Anjelica saw it the same way. "The most truly

comic moments in life come out of complete de-
vout seriousness," she said, commenting on the
contrast between the essential darkness of the
story and its comic potential. Her Maerose was a
woman totally serious about one thing—getting
Charley Partanna back. It's the events along the
way that are comic.

But Nicholson saw nothing comic in the book
Huston gave him to read. He went down to Puerto
Vallarta to talk to Huston about the project. But
what they did mostly, Nicholson recalled, was sit
around watching the Olympic boxing matches on
TV. Nicholson would bring up the book, telling
Huston that the jokes needed to be rewritten. Huston listened to everything Nicholson said and
made no comment. And then finally he said, "Well,
you know, it's a comedy."

Once Nicholson understood that the comic
values of the story lay in the contrasts between the
nature of the plot—boy loses girl, boy meets girl,
boy and girl fall in love, boy and girl fall out, boy
goes back to first girl—and the bizarre characters
playing it rather than in any set "jokes," he went
to work developing Charley Partanna.

Both Anjelica and Nicholson had their doubts
about playing in the film. Anjelica realized that
ABC Motion Pictures, for whom Foreman produced the film, might well have wanted a better-
known actress for the key role she played. After
all, she had not even tested for the part. And she
had to hold her own with Kathleen Turner, a major threat in any league. "But the fact that I was
my father's daughter and Jack's girlfriend, there

was nothing much they could do about ousting me." Still, her own sense of self told her that she brought something important to the picture. "It might seem to many people that I am privileged to be in this company," she said. "And I certainly doubt that I would have been in *Prizzi's Honor* had neither of them been a part of it. On the other hand, I feel I was instrumental in making it happen."

As indeed she was. Is there anyone else for whom Jack Nicholson would have risked abandoning the intelligent roles he had always had and appearing as a rather dumb hired killer?

And at one point it looked as though the risk also included wearing a wig. Huston said to Nicholson that "everything you've done until now has been intelligent. We can't have any of that in this film." He wanted audiences who had seen Nicholson in other roles such as the astronaut in *Terms of Endearment* to know that *Prizzi's Honor* was different from anything Nicholson had ever done—and to know it from the first time he came on screen. To accomplish this, Huston suggested that Nicholson wear a wig.

Nicholson understood what Huston wanted to achieve, but his initial reaction was that there must be something that would have the same effect without running the risk of making his character look older than he is supposed to be. The device he finally used—the particular way he curled his mouth throughout the film—came to him one day while he and John Huston toured Brooklyn, the setting for the movie, with some friends. Nicholson practiced using his mouth the way he wanted to—this involved padding under the lip— and tried it out on Huston one day.

"Oh, fine," Huston said. "No wig."

Adding a Brooklyn accent to the curled lip made Charley Partanna completely different from any other role Nicholson had played. But at least his audiences knew he didn't always look or talk that way. Few people had seen Anjelica, so when the elegant and beautiful Maerose opened her mouth and out came that wonderful working-class Brooklyn accent, many—including a lot of people in the movie industry—thought Anjelica must talk that way in real life. In fact, Anjelica says, her agent still gets calls from producers asking if Anjelica really has a Brooklyn accent.

Of course, Anjelica says, Maerose's accent attracted even more attention coming out of a woman who, even at home, "gets up in the morning, puts on the full stick, and stays that way." Anjelica said that Maerose is typical of a lot of women who live the same way. Referring to Gina Lollobrigida, the Italian actress, with whom she appeared in a seminar, Anjelica said, "You can tell from looking at her that she gets up every morning, puts on her makeup, perfects her hair and nails—creates herself. It's something many of the old-time movie stars had, and it's very much Maerose. She has a knot in her heart, but she's going to look and be her best. I think it shows a lot of self-respect. It's the kind of thing that wins the war."

To John Huston the accents were what made

Prizzi's Honor work. To hear some of the outrageous things that were said about killing in that distinctive way somehow made everyone realize that this can be laughed at—this is funny. And to achieve that effect, Huston brought in dialogue coach Julie Bavasso (who coached the actors for their accents in the film *Moonstruck* and who played Cher's aunt in that film), who read some of the script to the cast and then worked with them until their accents sounded real. "When you use a dialect, you worry that the people you're imitating will think you're making fun of them," Jack Nicholson said. "But we eventually got it together."

And Anjelica did especially well. One reviewer said of Anjelica's Maerose, "She has created a grand grotesque—Lucrezia Borgia with a Brooklyn accent, Iago in high heels."

But it wasn't easy.

The memory of that first disastrous film must have haunted Anjelica at least a little bit. When *A Walk With Love and Death* was released early in 1969, it found almost universal audience and critical apathy. At least one reviewer, Pauline Kael, found this "romantic idyll . . . unusually tough-minded, and effective because it is." But Kael stood pretty much alone, and although John Huston, used to failures and already involved in another project, found it easy to shake off the failure of his daughter's first film, Anjelica didn't. It would be sixteen years before she was ready to work with him again, and during those years her father would maintain a hands-off policy toward his daughter's life and career that mirrors another famous father-children relationship, that of Henry Fonda with his children, Peter and Jane.

Peter Fonda commented once that he asked Anjelica if her father had given her much advice about acting, or taken much interest in her work. "No," Anjelica told him. "He lives in a castle, we live in a gatehouse."

She was referring to St. Clerans, the Irish castle where she and brother Tony grew up. At first they lived in the estate's gatehouse, since the castle had to undergo extensive renovation and repair. But even after it was finished, Anjelica's mother preferred living in the smaller place, leaving to John Huston the role of lord of the manor, which he played while in residence to a never-ending stream of famous guests.

Prizzi's Honor presented the opportunity to close the distance, both personal and artistic, that separated father and daughter for all time. And one of the happiest moments for Anjelica during the filming came when she realized that she and her father both saw Maerose the same way, and that her performance was right on track.

It happened the day Anjelica and the costume designer worked on her dress for the wedding reception in the opening scenes of the movie. "I was . . . trying on a dress that was black with a frilly taffeta piece that came over the shoulder and looped to the other side: a designer dress from the Fifties . . . I told . . . our designer . . . I thought it would be interesting to take off the ruffle and drape it in Schiaparelli pink. . . . Just then my father entered the room. He looked at me and the dress and said, 'Well, what do you think about making the ruffle in Schiaparelli pink!' That was the moment I knew there was no separation in the way we saw the character."

Although Maerose's dress in her first scene is pure Fifties, it's almost impossible to tell from other details in the costumes and setting whether the story takes place in the Fifties, the Eighties, or somewhere in between. And that was exactly the effect John Huston wanted to create, according to production designer Dennis Washington. He wanted the film to float somewhere in time, perhaps in order to increase audience perception that this is a fairy story, this doesn't really happen—it's okay to laugh.

That desire presented Washington with some tricky problems. For example, New York City police cars became blue and white in 1971: before that, they were green. To make the cars seem to come from "somewhere in time," old cars were repainted in new colors. Finally, Washington and set decorator Bruce Weintraub and costume designer Donfeld decided to use the year 1962 as a point of reference from which to take their creative inspiration.

Commented Weintraub about 1962: "It was a fun period, full of Formica and plastic and artificial flowers. It was the Sixties—but not. It was before the 'enlightenment' of the Sixties. Maerose and Charley are about as far from Woodstock as you're gonna get!"

A further complication was that Maerose is an interior decorator: she has designed both her own apartment and Charley's, so these places must be seen through her eyes. "Charley's place is 'Bill Blassian' as interpreted by Maerose," said Weintraub, citing the houndstooth chairs on black-and-white-checkered floors, the black-and-white bedsheets.

Maerose's occupation is another instance of art imitating life: although Anjelica Huston has never been a decorator, she has the same love for beautiful things as her father had, and she says that is one of his most important legacies to her. Huston himself said, "Anjelica has a rare appreciation of things done with a certain amount of style. Those periods of my life where style was most evident she refers to most often."

In her own life Anjelica pays a great deal of attention to style. She lives in a small pink house furnished with her own treasured things, including needlepoint pillows her mother embroidered in the last years of her marriage to John Huston and a collection of fans that her grandmother had given to her mother. Jack Nicholson lives just up the road from that little pink house, and for several years Anjelica lived in it with him. Then, she said, "It was necessary to remove myself from the entourage a career like his engenders. I had never lived alone. I didn't even know what color I liked my coffee in the morning."

But there is no such diffidence in Maerose. Maerose, as Anjelica saw and played her, is "a well-grounded girl . . . someone very real who came from a situation in which she had to fight and pull her own weight." Maerose, she says, "gets a full background, she doesn't just appear as tarantulan. We see what she has gone through—held down, ostracized, punished. That'll change you. We're all products of our upbringing."

By the time filming started, Anjelica could draw not only on her longtime relationship with Jack Nicholson, but on her newfound relationship with her father. Talking about her first scene with Nicholson at the wedding reception, a scene in which Maerose makes it plain that she hasn't gotten over him, and in which Charley tells her to solve her problems by "practicing her meatballs," Anjelica recalled that she needed a "particular frame of mind for Maerose." She says she looked around at some latticework framing the set and "saw two perfect ovals. Jack was behind one and my father was behind the other. I could literally look from one to the other and use it for Maerose."

She used it well. Terence Rafferty, writing in the Autumn 1985 *Sight and Sound*, said "Anjelica Huston's face is the last image in the movie before the credits roll. John Huston seems to have chosen his daughter to stand in for him this time, to represent on screen the family traits: a combination of philosophical fatalism—the let's-see-what-happens passivity which has sometimes made Huston's actors very uncomfortable—and a steely determination to get exactly what one wants."

The line that goes with the image—Maerose's wonderful Brooklyn voice charged with triumph and desire saying, "Holy cow, Charley, where do ya wanna meet?"—brings the film to a satisfying conclusion, the ending such a story had to have.

That ending made another beginning—the beginning of the glory road for Anjelica. She won the New York Film Critics Award. She won the Los Angeles Film Critics Award. She won an Academy Award for Best Supporting Actress. And in winning that Oscar, she helped John Huston to another "first." He had already earned the accolade of being the first director to direct his own father to an Oscar—Walter Huston in *The Treasure of the Sierra Madre*. Now he had also directed his daughter to the same award.

The nomination for an Oscar was "a fairy tale come true for the three of us," Anjelica said when that happened, the three of course being herself, her father, and Jack. Although she thought being nominated was like a dream, it also gave her nightmares. "I have this vision of the guy in the movie *The Oscar* jumping up when he hears someone else's name. I want to make sure that I've got a strong arm beside me to keep me down should that happen."

The film was also up for Best Movie, Huston was up for Best Director, and Nicholson was up for Best Actor. But on Oscar night it was Anjelica's party, all the way. She went to the ceremonies knowing that "whether or not you get it, there'll be tears before bedtime. Too much fun at the fair." Jack Nicholson was right beside her—but he didn't need to use that strong arm to hold her down. There was no mistake—it was Anjelica's name that was called.

If there were any tears, no one saw them, and Anjelica only remembers that she "had a wonderful time that night. After the Governor's Ball we went to Dad's hotel room," she said. "Everyone was a bit pissed off that he [her father] didn't get it, but I wasn't going to allow that to spoil my parade. I knew he and Jack would've preferred I win, rather than the flip. That was comforting." And even though Anjelica says the whole business of the Oscar is insane, that you can't compare one actor to another—still, as she admits, "You want it."

That Oscar also taught Anjelica one of Hollywood's most contradictory lessons: an Oscar is not an automatic entrée to other parts. Three days after she received her award for Best Supporting Actress, Anjelica tried for a role in *Witches of Eastwick*—and lost out to Cher. In fact, such a quick succession of triumph and failure is also in the Huston motif: John Huston, with his "gambler's mix of heedlessness, ego, and fatalism," was "just about impervious to failure." He had far more flops than he had hits over his long career, but still, he made a film nearly every year for over forty years, among them some of the most memorable and remarkable movies ever made: *The Maltese Falcon*, *The African Queen*, and *The Treasure of the Sierra Madre*.

Prizzi's Honor turned out to be one of Huston's hits. It had all the ingredients that, mixed by a director of John Huston's skill, blend into a pastiche full of surprises. Where else is there a movie that, very close to its end, presents as startling and graphic a murder as any ever filmed—and still sends audiences out laughing?

Perhaps one reason the film works so well is that since John Huston believed a director should be able to get what he wants on the first take, the film had a spontaneous feeling that made the humor that much fresher. Jack Nicholson recalled that he had never made a movie with so many one-take scenes as *Prizzi's Honor*, and Anjelica found the situation unsettling at first because her father did not give them a lot of feedback.

But Huston's method, which barred going over and over a scene until there were no surprises left, provided Anjelica with a memorable moment she might otherwise not have had. Speaking of a scene with William Hickey, who played her grandfather, the Don, Anjelica said, "I had wondered how he would deliver the stultifying line 'You are flesh of my flesh, blood of my blood.' . . . I walked in and kissed his ring. Then he stood up, did a little dance, and said, in a funny little voice, 'You are flesh of my flesh, blood of my blood.' He did it with such joy, such effervescence, and such affection toward me that I completely understood who I was: I'm his little girl and he's my grandpa who makes me laugh."

She might have been speaking of Walter Huston, the grandfather she never knew, who died shortly after John Huston and her mother, ballerina Ricki Soma, were married. Walter Huston had that capacity for joy, and a genuine affection for people, that made him very different from his son. Walter would have adored Anjelica, and she would have adored him. Through that brief scene with the Don, she could use some of that wish for connection with the past.

In a way *Prizzi's Honor* formed a major link between Anjelica's past and her future. It was a peak experience for her, one in which all the forces of her life came together—father, lover, past, present—and from which she emerged ready to assume the legacy to which her father was putting the finishing touches. That legacy would be completed during the filming of John Huston's last film, *The Dead*, in which Anjelica starred.

It was a short enough road between *Prizzi's Honor* and *The Dead*, finished in the spring of 1987, several months before Huston's death on August 28 of that year. But it had been a very long road between Anjelica's birth in July of 1951, while her father shot *The African Queen*, his classic film starring Humphrey Bogart and Katharine Hepburn, and the day Anjelica was asked to play Maerose.

That road begins long before her birth. It begins, in fact, with the birth of her grandfather, Walter Huston, in whose genes the theatrical legacy came to life in the first place.

CHAPTER 2

"*T*HE song is over, but the melody lingers on . . ." might well be applied to Walter Huston's memory, particularly since his rendition of "September Song" is still heard every time a VCR owner rents the Joan Fontaine–Joseph Cotten classic, *September Affair*. From all accounts the elder Huston was one of those people whose immense talent did not get in the way of his humanity: he was universally loved, and although high-spirited, never indulged in the kind of antics that led the crew of one of John Huston's films to nickname him Double Ugly.

Walter Huston was Canadian by birth, born in

Toronto, Canada, in 1884 into a family that on his Irish father's side went back to the thirteenth century. Huston's mother Elizabeth was Scottish. Two daughters, Nan and Margaret, and another son, Alec, completed the family. The creative arts apparently ran in the family: when Walter's father, Robert Huston, died suddenly when the children were still young, the oldest brother, Alec, earned a living for the family by painting signs and inventing things. Thanks to his efforts, Nan studied piano and became a teacher, and Margaret, whose life among the rich and famous would later inspire nephew John to aspire to the same sort of style, studied singing. The ladies of Toronto raised enough money to send Margaret to Paris at age eighteen for further study, and from there she launched a career as a dramatic soprano that would have positive repercussions in the lives of other family members.

As with so many imaginative youngsters, Walter's acting aspirations first manifested themselves in his making up plays at home, fashioning costumes out of whatever came to hand. By his late teens Walter was on the road with a repertory company, and although life in a struggling rep company touring the provinces of Canada at the turn of the century posed hardship, it also provided the best possible training for an aspiring actor. Only in a rep company does the least novice have an opportunity to act the larger roles: furthermore, the demands of learning many roles quickly, of going from one to the other as the bill changes, give invaluable training in memory and characterization. The discipline and creativity that made Walter Huston such a standout later were laid down on the muddy, hungry road.

Tours with other rep companies, all of which eventually went broke, and a brief stint in New York were followed by another tour, this one with a company touring a play called *The Sign of the Cross*. One stop on the tour was the St. Louis World's Fair—and there Walter Huston met Rhea Gore, the woman who became his first wife and John Huston's mother.

Rhea's father, John Gore, had served the Confederacy as a drummer boy. He married an Ohio girl, Adelia Richardson, and rode a thoroughbred horse in the Oklahoma Land Rush, when he who got there first could stake his claim to land. An adventurer, John Gore moved as the land opened, setting up newspapers in townlet after townlet— and getting others to pay for the presses to print them. Land wars were common, gunplay routine. To get daughter Rhea into safer territory, her mother put her in a convent school in St. Louis.

Marriage to Walter took Rhea right back out west: the farther west they went, the more dangerous the situation became, with concrete-minded audiences waiting at the stage door to beat up the play's villain, and sheriff's posses following them out of town to recover the receipts. Broke and stranded, Walter and Rhea went to Nevada, Missouri, where John and Adelia Gore lived, John having won the town's light-power-and-water company at the poker table.

Walter took the job as chief engineer of his father-in-law's company, and on August 5, 1906, John Huston was born. Several other such jobs followed, taking the family to Indianapolis and Weatherford, Texas. But those Huston acting genes just wouldn't sit still, and when Walter's sister Margaret, now a successful singer, asked him to come to New York and follow the career he was meant for—he went. Thus, early on, John Huston learned the lesson that when art calls—all else goes, including wife and family.

The New York venture failed. Walter hated Margaret's lifestyle, finding her high-class friends dull. She, in turn, found her brother provincial and given to loud, tasteless clothes. And while later in his life Walter Huston would have the world's great among those he called friend, and would move among them like one to the manor born, at that time he would have none of it. Back on the road, to the life he called playing "rep, tent, and tab," a life that took him to every city with as many as twenty thousand people, including places in mid-America where hotels had signs saying: NO DOGS OR ACTORS ALLOWED!

Eventually Walter teamed up with Bayonne Whipple, the woman he would marry next. They developed a headline act that worked: step-by-step Walter Huston and Bayonne Whipple made it to the top of vaudeville. And then, after fifteen years of acting in stock companies on the road and doing one song-and-dance routine after the other, Walter Huston, at forty years of age, appeared on Broadway, and a whole new chapter of the Huston saga began.

The role, that of Mr. Pitt in Zona Gale's play of the same name, led to another—and then came the biggest break of all. Margaret had by now married an older man whose millions came to her when he fell off a horse while riding in New York's Central Park. From her Park Avenue townhouse Margaret developed a whole new life in the arts, ranging from being a patron of the work of others to giving private elocution lessons to actors who attracted her attention.

Then in 1920, not long before Walter got the role in Gale's play, Margaret married Robert Edmond Jones, a scenic designer and director who was a close friend and associate of playwright Eugene O'Neill. (Interestingly enough, Margaret retained the name Carrington, that of her first husband, throughout her marriage to Jones. Rumored to be homosexual, Jones went off to a Swiss clinic for treatment during the marriage: whatever happened behind closed doors, Margaret and Jones were best of friends and had a solid marriage.)

In 1924, after Walter had had another role on Broadway, Bobby Jones introduced Walter to Eugene O'Neill, saying that he thought Walter would be perfect for the lead in O'Neill's new play, *Desire Under the Elms*. Originally resistant because Huston's two previous Broadway roles had been, in terms of the characteristics of the men he played, exactly the opposite of the central character in *Desire*, O'Neill finally gave in and allowed Huston to be cast. He never regretted the decision, saying later that only three actors ever realized his characters as he originally saw them, and that Walter Huston was one of them.

John Huston, who had come to New York that summer at age eighteen, might have learned another lesson then that later served him so well: Don't be afraid of casting that seems unlikely; it might be some of the best you've ever done. And watching rehearsals, John Huston absorbed another lesson as he watched O'Neill and Jones work. O'Neill never spoke to an actor out loud: he wrote notes and gave them to Jones, or he said something in such a low voice no one else could hear him. Huston would later be known for his intimate style of directing, the way he seemed to find the precise suggestion, given by note or in a low, personal tone, that would send an actor or actress on exactly the right path to the character's heart.

Desire Under the Elms wasn't understood by most of the reviewers, and it was denounced by minister after minister, with at least one newspaper demanding it be shut down as offensive and salacious. The mayor of New York sent a committee to review the play—their verdict was that it was a work of art.

But dirt, not art, sold the tickets that kept *Desire* running for half a year and put Walter Huston in the money for the first time in his acting career.

This was a heady time for the Huston clan. Margaret, clearly the head of the family, was "onstage" from the moment the first guest walked into the room in any of her lavish homes to the time the door closed behind the last one. Even among the brilliant company she gathered around her dinner table, she shone, being described in the *New Republic* as one of the "half dozen most distinguished and brilliant figures of the last two decades."

The richness of Margaret's houses, the lavishness of her table, impressed nephew John—years later, when he purchased his castle in Ireland, he would duplicate a life he first observed in his Aunt Margaret's homes. Something else he inherited from her: the charisma that made her the center of attention in any gathering. Everybody watched Margaret, John Huston recalled, adding that he admired her but didn't particularly like to be around her. Because she took all the attention for herself?

Walter Huston's career went into overdrive after *Desire Under the Elms* and stayed there. He would be in demand in the motion picture industry for the rest of his life, and his son John would find many doors opened to the next generation of Huston talent by his father's generous hand. Nor would the generosity be unreturned: Walter Huston won his Oscar when directed by his son in the classic *The Treasure of the Sierra Madre,* one of the films John Huston continued to watch whenever it happened to appear on late-night TV years after he no longer wanted to see his earlier work.

Walter Huston's marriage to Bayonne Whipple ended soon after his first New York success: he married once more, to Nan Sunderland, the woman he was still married to at his death. An actress, Nan met Walter in New York, and after their marriage both went out to Hollywood and set up housekeeping there. *A House Divided*, a film on the order of *Desire Under the Elms*, starred Walter Huston—and gave John his first crack at script-writing. Although the younger Huston made only a small contribution to the finished script, he did make valuable contacts. Throughout his life Walter Huston helped his son whenever he could, from getting H. L. Mencken, editor of the renowned *American Mercury* magazine, to read John Huston's short story titled "Fool"—Mencken published it—to steering him into jobs in Hollywood. And although Rhea and Walter divorced when John was still a child, Walter kept in contact with him, bringing him more and more into his life until, from about age eighteen on, John was much more in his father's circle than his mother's.

A pattern that John would repeat with his own children—and one that bears out the truism that people rear their children in the way they themselves were reared, repeating not only the good things, but those not so good as well. The difference, of course, is in the person using the pattern. Walter Huston, a kind and generous man, kept giving John a hand even after he failed over and over again. John would be thirty-six before he made any mark at all in Hollywood—but no matter what he needed, whether it was money or an introduction or a job, or just love and support, he got it from his father. Years later John would give daughter Anjelica a chance at an acting career when he starred her in *A Walk With Love and Death* when she was sixteen. But after that failure it would be nineteen years before he held his hand out to her again.

Walter was the kind of parent who gave approval freely, never openly criticizing, only frowning if his son said or did something he thought wrong. But he gave John an amazing amount of latitude, considering the antics John indulged in from his first days in Hollywood. Walter commented once to an interviewer from *Look* magazine that although his son was a wild Indian, he had always known he was something special.

And John returned that affection and respect, saying after his father's death in 1950 that they had been as close as father and son could be. Obviously one of the strongest bases for this closeness lay in the fact that they were both devoted to and exceptionally good at the theatrical arts. Even people who are not blood kin develop a family feeling when they work together in a play or a movie: there is something about having moments of creative satisfaction occur within that group that makes a bond. And time and time again Walter and John Huston worked on the same project as Walter's career soared and John's started the first slow slope of his climb to the top.

Another bond between Walter and John was their love for a good joke, and their willingness to pursue the absurd, all in the cause of a laugh. They constantly played jokes upon one another, and one of their time-honored games was a contest in which he who made the other laugh first won. It could also be ego-bruising, John Huston recalled, to be setting out deliberately to make a fool of yourself so as to crack up your father and have him sit like the Great Stone Face all the while. One highly successful ploy John Huston remembered well. The contest had been going on for some time, with neither able to make the other laugh. Finally John had an inspiration. He went into the bedroom and stripped off all his clothes, returning to the living room clad only in neckties. One tied around each ankle, more tied around each wrist, one wrapped around his forehead— and one other, tied in a prominently obvious place. "Dad laughed," John said.

That sense of the ridiculous livened moments on the set, too. John Huston's first directorial assignment, the movie that would become a bench mark of his career and a classic of its kind, *The Maltese Falcon*, was the beginning of a Walter Huston tradition—to appear in each of his son's movies as a kind of good luck charm.

Walter played the captain who arrives in Sam Spade's office, hands him the package containing the Maltese falcon, and then collapses dead on the rug. For an actor of Walter's skill, the scene, including the death fall, should have been a piece of cake. But John kept shooting the scene over and over again, until his father, bruised and sore, rebelled.

Never one to let a good joke die, John enlisted Mary Astor, who costarred with Humphrey Bogart in the film, to call his father the next morning, pretending to be the producer's secretary. She told Walter that the lab had somehow messed up the film from the day's takes, and that he would have to come back so the scene could be shot again. Walter's reply, yelled into the mouthpiece and heard by everyone at the other end, told his son to get another actor or to go to hell. After taking twenty falls, Walter shouted, he had had enough.

The tradition of always appearing in his son's films didn't always hold, although Walter did appear in many of them. Often his own career commitments conflicted with John's film schedule. And as John began to shoot more and more on location, acting for him in bit parts became impractical.

But Walter did appear in his son's first film shot on location, *The Treasure of the Sierra Madre*, shot in the wilds of Mexico at a time when every other director and producer relied on sets built back at the Hollywood studios.

From the moment John Huston read the B. Traven novel on which the classic film is based, he had seen the role of Howard, the old sourdough, as absolutely perfect for his dad. (Just as Maerose Prizzi, years and years later, would be absolutely perfect for daughter Anjelica? Ironically—or, considering John Huston's imaginative and intuitive powers, not ironically at all—the roles led to Academy Awards for both Walter Huston and Anjelica.)

Walter even took out his teeth to play the part, at John's request, a sort of forerunner of John's idea that Jack Nicholson perhaps wear a wig in *Prizzi's Honor* to establish that this role was different from anything he had ever done. After all, up until this time Walter Huston had had leading-man roles—and the old prospector, Howard, is anything but the stereotypical leading man.

Even before the Academy Award voters acclaimed Walter, his son knew they had brought home a winner. "It was certainly the finest performance in any picture I ever made," John Huston said. "When he does that dance of triumph before the mountain . . . the gooseflesh comes out and my hair stands up: a tribute to greatness that has happened, with me, in the presence of [the great Russian opera singer] Chaliapin, the Italian thoroughbred Ribot, Jack Dempsey in his prime, and Manolete."

A tribute few fathers—or actors—can match.

Toward the end of the filming of *Treasure,* word came that Walter's brother, Alec, who'd been living in a small town in Canada, had died. That brought on a round of reminiscing as the two Irishmen "waked" their dead home. John had gone to see his uncle the previous year. What Alec had wanted to hear about wasn't John's experiences in World War II as a member of the Army Special Services—he had made three documentaries during his military stint—but about a colossal fight John and Errol Flynn had had at a David Selznick party that had put them both in the hospital—and made them fast friends.

Apparently the "outrageous genes" were firmly embedded in the Huston family: Alec's daughter Margaret told them later that at the very end of her father's life, a second cousin came out from Toronto to see him. Alec refused, saying the woman was a bore, and that he didn't have to waste even one of the last hours of his life on her. No amount of entreaty would change his mind, and the way they finally got rid of the cousin was to have Margaret tell her Alec had died. When the cousin came in to see the "corpse," Alec played dead until she left. His actual death came a few days after this typically Huston death scene, staged with total disregard for the proprieties—but a great deal of regard for personal style.

Walter impressed others besides his son during the filming of *Treasure.*

Humphrey Bogart, who played the lead role of Fred C. Dobbs in the film, talked about his experience filming *Treasure* in a *Hollywood Reporter* interview in September 1947: "Every so often you get your teeth into a part and this was it. John wanted us to go down into Mexico . . . We went high into the mountains more than one hundred miles north of Distrito Federal . . . It was the damnedest location I ever was on . . . We'd stumble over rocks and stones and cactus and sagebrush. We'd dodge snakes and scorpions and things that must have been Gila monsters . . . And who do you think was the guy who made with the laughs and the quips and told us 'youngsters' to 'chin up, stout fellah'? Walter Huston, of course!"

Critics, too, praised Walter Huston, calling his performance "his best job in a lifetime of acting." The pièce de résistance, of course, was Oscar night, when Walter Huston won the award for the Best Supporting Actor and son John won the award for Best Director. The party to celebrate the Oscars, held at John Huston's ranch, featured a no-holds-barred football game with a genuine Ming vase for the ball. John wore his pet monkey Liberty around his neck, and the tuxedo-garbed players wreaked havoc on the room and on themselves. Ida Lupino sprained her back and a producer broke two ribs. To any but those in the profession, such wild swings from high art to low comedy seem crazy and irresponsible. But they all spring from the same source—the creative child that sees art in life and absurdity everywhere—even in a love affair between two professional killers like Charley Partanna and Irene Walker.

Although Walter Huston married three times, he did not have a reputation as a womanizer. He kept in touch with Rhea, his first wife, until after his second marriage, to Bayonne Whipple in 1915. And then the breach was of her doing. Her father, living in San Francisco at the time, and with yet another adventurous scheme in the works, asked his former son-in-law and the new bride to stay with him while he enlisted Walter's help in pulling off the plan. Rhea blamed her father for asking them, but her relations with her former husband cooled after that.

She had a career of her own by that time, however; she had begun work as a newspaper reporter two years before she divorced Walter in 1912. John traveled with his mother during those years, but although he remembers the experience with pleasure, years after Rhea's death he still said that she had never approved of him her whole life long. Rhea remarried, too, wedding Howard Eveleth

Stevens, who became a vice president of the Northern Pacific Railroad, and who at the time of their marriage was a widower with two small children of his own. He lived in Miriam Park, a suburb of St. Paul, Minnesota. In the Stevenses' home John Huston got his first taste of a conventional life. In view of the way he lived later, apparently a small taste proved enough.

Probably the most impulsive act Walter Huston ever did in his relationships with women was to obtain a quickie Las Vegas divorce from Bayonne so he could marry Nan Sunderland. They would remain happily married for almost twenty years, until Huston's death.

But his own ability to maintain one relationship at a time—although obviously he ended his marriage to Bayonne to embark on one with Nan—did not lead him to criticize his son's well-known inability to maintain one relationship at a time. John Huston would follow his father's example of multiple marriages, actually doubling Walter's record with five of his own. But from all reports, the marriage vow never kept him from straying from the marriage bed—often very soon after he was wed.

Still, Walter supported his son through the four marriages he witnessed before his death. He had been particularly supportive of John's first marriage, to Dorothy Jeanne Harvey, sending the young couple money during the frequent times they were broke. But even then, Walter's attitude was marked by a sort of laissez-faire, live-and-let-live approach that probably was responsible in large part for the closeness he maintained with his son.

Years later, when third wife Evelyn Keyes found herself being eased out so John could marry wife number four—Enrica Soma, who would be the mother of his first child—Walter told Keyes that she didn't have to try to explain what life with John Huston was like. "John has always been a bit of a free soul," he said, adding that he would tell her something for what it was worth. "When he married the first time," Walter said, "he was twenty and broke, and I gave him five hundred dollars to set up housekeeping. That was a lot of money then. He spent the entire amount on a chandelier." Walter gave Keyes a moment to think that over, then said, "I haven't worried about him too much since then."

When John married for the second time, to Leslie Black, his father, like most of the rest of John's friends, thought she was just what he needed to make a man of him. John had been too wild for too long—this English girl could help him find his best self and do the work he was always meant to do. But when John married for the third time, to Evelyn Keyes in a spur-of-the-moment ceremony that featured a ring found at the bottom of Mike Romanoff's swimming pool and an air charter flight to Las Vegas to tie the knot, Walter thought it a bad mistake. Still, when David Selznick and wife Jennifer Jones gave a huge party for the newlyweds, Walter Huston entertained the star-studded crowd of five hundred people with his famous "September Song," perhaps silently hoping that this marriage that seemed such a joke, just one more in a very long line of pranks staged by his rambunctious son, might actually see its way through into the quiet of December.

It didn't, of course. But by the time John went to Juárez, Mexico, to obtain an even quicker divorce from Evelyn than the one Walter got from Bayonne, the bride-to-be was seven months pregnant with the child who would be born just ten days after Walter Huston died. Time and time again, both in private histories and in the stories tracing the lives of the great, the significant juxtaposition of life and death, death and life, appear. Walter Huston died on April 6, 1950, his sixty-sixth birthday, thus taking out of John Huston's life one of the people most consistently important to it.

Walter had been in Los Angeles for a few days: a movie was in the offing, and he also wanted to check with the man who took care of his place in Running Springs. Son John planned a big celebration at Romanoff's, with a guest list that included old friends like Sam Spiegel (who would produce *The African Queen* for Huston the next year), Spencer Tracy, and Jed Harris, the famed Broadway producer and director who hated almost everyone in show business, but who adored Walter Huston.

Walter lunched with John's agent, Paul Kohner, and a few other people, and seemed fine. But several hours later he called John at the studio, where he was engaged in preproduction work on the filming of Stephen Crane's novel *The Red*

Badge of Courage, to say that he didn't feel well and had better skip the party. Since his father rarely begged off anything on the grounds of illness, John took this complaint seriously, particularly since the primary symptom was back pain so intense Walter almost passed out from it.

The Los Angeles doctors John called in thought Walter might have kidney stones; Walter's New York doctor, when consulted by telephone, thought Walter might have an aneurysm of the aorta. Giving their patient something for pain, the doctors left, planning to return in the morning. They let Walter stay at the hotel, believing that he would be better off without being moved, especially since John had taken a room right across the hall, and Walter's caretaker and a hotel porter would stay in the room with their patient that night.

The caretaker roused John in the middle of the night to say that his father was unconscious, and although the two doctors came right away, there was nothing to be done. Except for a brief flicker of recognition, a brief squeeze of his son's hand, Walter Huston remained unconscious until he died around eight o'clock the next morning.

Nan Huston had been out of town: she flew in six hours after her husband's death, which an autopsy proved to have been caused directly by internal bleeding and heart failure, both precipitated by an aneurysm of the aorta, just as the New York doctor had diagnosed. The surgical techniques that some years later saved John Huston from just the sort of vascular accident that killed his father came too late to save Walter. But at least his death was quick. As John said, "Dad was too tough to get sick. He just died, that's all. He went fast, the way he wanted to go."

Spencer Tracy delivered the eulogy at Walter Huston's memorial service, held at Hollywood's Academy Award Theatre. Calling Walter Huston "the best," Tracy said that while there was "nothing odd about being the top man in a profession . . . there is something odd if the top man happens to be the nicest . . . all the days we knew him, Walter Huston had a gentle mind, and he had the only thing that makes such a virtue endurable . . . he had the strength to quietly oppose the things that were wrong."

John Huston wrote his own eulogy to his father in his autobiography, *An Open Book*. He amplifies on the quality Tracy called "nice," saying that his father had "none of the hard edges associated with most 'personalities.'" Walter Huston never tried to come out the winner in either a business transaction or a personal relationship, nor did he ever raise his voice in anger in his son's hearing. In fact, over all their years together, in the business and out of it, John never heard his father take anyone to task, either to their faces or away from them.

Everyone felt comfortable with Walter Huston, and they showed it by going to him for advice and instruction. They could rely on his advice to be without self-interest: Walter Huston was simply too nice a guy to take advantage of anyone. And when he felt a situation warranted more than just advice, he worked behind the scenes to help. John relates the story of a time when his father urged him to have an answering service, despite the fact that John always had a servant at the house to answer the telephone. Walter persisted, mystifying his son, who kept refusing. Only years after Walter died did John learn his father's real reason for the request. An old friend of his, a woman whose acting career never really got off the ground, was on her uppers, and Walter had suggested that she begin an answering service. The first in Los Angeles, it became a great success. But in the beginning Walter went out drumming up business—and typically, would not burden even his son with his own altruistic motives.

Walter Huston's death ended a relationship that meant more than any other to his son. Rhea Huston never gave her son approval: Walter Huston never gave him disapproval. "Dad neither corrected nor criticized me when I was a child, but I always knew when I did something that displeased him—a vertical line appeared on his forehead," John said, adding that since he preferred to see his father laugh, he tried to avoid making that line appear.

A man of many skills and interests, Walter Huston was good at everything he tried. The one real failure came when he attempted a lifelong dream—to play a role from Shakespeare on the stage. With Nan playing Desdemona, Walter played Othello in a Central City, Colorado, production of the Shakespeare tragedy. When the production was a hit, Robert Edmond Jones,

Margaret Huston Carrington's second husband, brought it to New York.

John felt uneasy from the moment he saw the Philadelphia tryout. The production overpowered the performance—"One came away with a sense more of spectacle rather than drama," said one critic. And although opening night in New York's Amsterdam Theatre brought Walter an ovation, still, John had his doubts. The reviews bore him out.

John went over to the Waldorf Towers, and to his father's room, thinking to be with him when he first read the bad reviews. From the hall outside John could hear his father laughing. The reviews would stop that, John thought. Until he got inside and saw that his father had read the reviews, and that laughter was his response to the dream of a lifetime vanishing down the same critical tube where those of so many others before him had gone.

Still, Walter had played his dream and played it to a live audience, the acting situation he loved best of all. Both Hustons agreed that only through playing to a live audience, appearing in the same part night after night, can the actor smooth and shape his characterization until it reaches the ideal. Movie actors don't have time to do this with a role, so they must often resort to devices, tricks that fool the eye of the casual observer, but that do not fool the actor himself.

Walter Huston had the ability, which not all actors have, to transform himself, to become the person he was playing. He also kept a core of humanity, the thing that made him, in his son's opinion, have "an inborn politeness and respect for others." This rare combination of consummate artist and compassionate human being left a monumental mark, both in the acting world and in the private world of Walter Huston's personal relationships.

"There was no one else with whom I would laugh in the same way or share the same freedom," John Huston said about the loss of his father. Those last two words—"same freedom"— seem a poignant key to the kind of relationships John Huston sought all of his life. He and his father *were* free. After his divorce from Rhea, Walter chose to stay in his son's life, and to give him constant approval and support.

Nor did John have the kind of responsibility for his father that some highly successful people do. He need pay no bills for him, manufacture no parts for him. He did not have to comfort him through a long and debilitating last illness, nor watch while his father slowly lost the faculties that made him such a life-lover—and life-giver.

A rare situation indeed—all that love, and no responsibility attached. John Huston had experienced such a relationship since early childhood. It is small wonder that in other adult relationships he seemed to keep thinking he would stumble on such again.

John Huston told a story about his father that perfectly captures Walter Huston's special spirit. Walter, Nan, John, and a companion of his had gone on a picnic, stopping at a field of wildflowers and getting out to admire the blooms. All of a sudden Walter Huston bent down and began pounding a flower into the ground with his fist. Although this was but one flower out of millions, it shocked the rest of them all the same. Walter pounded more flowers—and then jumped up and down, prancing in an ever-widening circle, stamping flowers into the ground. He reminded John of no one so much as the Great God Pan—and when Nan asked him what on earth he thought he was doing, Walter replied just as that manic god might have. "I'm stopping the spring!" he said.

On April 6, 1950, when Walter Huston died, he stopped that spring for all who loved him.

CHAPTER 3

*J*OHN Marcellus Huston was born on August 5, 1906, in Nevada, Missouri, the town whose power-water-and-light company his grandfather had won in a poker game. Gambling ran in the Gore blood: John Huston's main legacy from his mother Rhea was a love of horses and a love of gambling, a love that alternately plagued him and rewarded him all his life. Rhea's no-nonsense approach to life countered Walter's creative imagination. She told young John when he was five that there was no Easter bunny, but his legacy from his father was stronger. There was magic in the world, and John Huston spent a lifetime proving it.

Viewed as an artist, Huston was an amazing talent who could write, paint, box, ride, act, direct—and charm almost anyone into doing almost anything. Producer Dore Schary said once that when John wanted you to do something, he would sit next to you and start talking in that low voice, his attention wholly on you—and before you knew what had happened, you had agreed to whatever it was he had in mind. Katharine Hepburn, who met him for the first time when they worked together on *The African Queen*, said that when John was in the room, all attention focused on him. "Just as it does on a small child," she added. But by the time they finished filming the movie, even Hepburn was squarely in the Huston camp, stating that she had never had a director who could so quickly and succinctly indicate to her how a part should be played. "He told me to put on a smile like Mrs. Roosevelt . . . a sort of chin up, the best is yet to come sort of smile. . . . That is the goddamnedest best piece of direction I have ever heard. I was his from there on in," she said.

Other Hollywood greats felt the same way. Orson Welles summed up the Huston persona with these few words: "Huston played Mephistopheles to his own Faust." A highly perceptive statement, which acknowledges the conflicts most geniuses experience. One part of them wants to be human, the other wants to be divine. Huston could never decide which, so his life was a series of complications, not necessarily for him, but for those involved with him.

Kirk Douglas commented, after Huston's

death on August 28, 1987, that if anything, Huston might have been too talented. "He could have been a great artist, he could have been a writer, he could have been an actor, and he was a great director." Douglas also said that when John wanted to be, he could be a bit of a charlatan, arranging, for example, scenes of films he was shooting to take place in Ireland when they really didn't have to be so that he could be at St. Clerans, his castle there. And, adds Douglas, "You never said no to John. He had the charm to seduce man, woman, and beast."

So how did John Huston go from a rather transient childhood, parented by a mother who never approved of him and a father who approved of him but who was never there, to "Great Man" status, acquiring five wives along the way, and lovers too numerous to count? A combination of that talent, that charm—pushes and lifts from his father—smiles from Lady Luck on a couple of occasions—and luck Huston made on many others. Huston's story has a lot in common with other famous people's, but as always, the story is individual, too.

His first taste of the theater came in 1924, when he spent his eighteenth summer in a New York apartment, watching his father rehearse *Desire Under the Elms* and appearing in a Sherwood Anderson comedy, *The Triumph of the Egg*, himself. By the next summer he had married Dorothy Jeanne Harvey, a girl no one seems to remember, and whom John left almost immediately when he went to Mexico for an extended adventure there. The marriage was still on—it wouldn't end until 1933—but it was marriage John Huston style, which meant he was away a lot, and Dorothy was left on her own. In fairness, it was marriage Hollywood style, too. Dorothy intended to be a writer, but in the meantime she enjoyed the perks of being married to Huston, who by now had a job at Universal Studios as a writer. They fell in with a set that did a great deal of sailing—and a great deal of drinking. Dorothy had a maid, played tennis, had her hair done, went to lunch with other movie industry wives—and forgot about writing.

John forgot about keeping the marriage vows: the affairs were casual, Hollywood-style things— until Dorothy walked into the wrong room and caught him. It had apparently never entered her mind that John would be unfaithful, despite the fact that the crowd they ran with was rife with infidelities. Already a heavy drinker—the martini shaker came out when John's foot hit the door— she now retired into the bottle, trying to reconstruct that perfect world she had lived in through alcohol.

Huston dealt with Dorothy's alcoholism by moving them to a beach house isolated from the old crowd. Neither would drink, he said, and she seemed to agree, even though like so many alcoholics she said she did not have a drinking problem. Before they moved to the beach, Dorothy would start drinking at five every day and drink until she passed out around midnight. Now, when Huston got home around five, she would already be drunk. At first he thought this was some psychological reaction to stopping drinking: her psyche was making her appear drunk. Then he discovered caches of bottles all over the house, bottles delivered by all sorts of people including their laundry man.

"There was a complete change of spirit in this woman whom I had only known to be warm, generous, loving, and full of the joy of living," John said. "Now she was withdrawn, and in her eyes I saw occasional flashes of resentment, perhaps hatred. I had become her jailer."

Some months later, "despite my feelings of guilt and responsibility," Huston said, "I decided to cut and run."

Dorothy left, too, sailing to England with an actress friend after filing for divorce, a suit that asked for nothing from John. But that was not yet the end of this unhappy situation.

John's life became further complicated when a girl ran out in front of him when he was driving from his father's house to Hollywood one night. John couldn't avoid hitting her—and the next day she died. He had not been drinking—a hitchhiker he'd just picked up verified that he had been going only about thirty miles an hour, and that the girl had run right out in front of him—but an earlier DWI and a night in jail during the drinking days had already marked him as reckless. Fed up with everything, John went to England, too, and there the last act of his first marriage played out.

Dorothy was drinking again, entertaining often, reliving the old Hollywood life. John stopped by to see her a couple of times, on one occasion buying an Irish Sweepstakes ticket from a man selling them. Then came the week he stopped by her flat three days in a row, only to receive no answer. Thinking she must have gone away for a few days, Huston waited, then returned later in the week. This time, although no one answered the door, he could hear Dorothy's dog crying. He called the manager, and they opened the door to find a half-starved dog and Dorothy passed out on the bed. Her chest had a burn mark the length of a cigarette. She'd been smoking when she passed out.

At the hospital she seemed all right at first, but early the next morning John found her much worse. In fact, they both believed that she was dying from the effects of the treatment the hospital had used. It involved strychnine, and though the chances of bad side effects were slim, this time the odds had gone against her. Her life was saved, and John took her over again, renting a small house and starting the no-drinking regime.

Dorothy didn't last long without alcohol, and on the heels of that crisis came a financial one: John got word from the British studio where he'd been working that he had broken his contract and was no longer on their payroll. Unable to work anywhere else in England without another permit, unwilling to cable his father for money, Huston didn't know what on earth he would do—until the doorbell rang again. The horses had saved him— not for the first time, and certainly not for the last. The ticket he'd bought in the Irish Sweepstakes

had won a one-hundred-pound consolation prize—
enough money at that time to buy a ticket home
for Dorothy. Before the day was over, Huston had
sent her back to California, where her parents
waited to take her in.

Peter Viertel, a writer who worked with Huston on various projects over the years including
The African Queen, wrote a novel titled *White
Hunter, Black Heart* that is reputed to be a very
thinly veiled portrait of John Huston. Not at all
flattering, the novel shows a lot of warts that the
Huston aura usually managed to conceal. But
there is a paragraph in it that might serve as a
kind of epitaph for John and Dorothy's marriage:

> I knew I had lost the best dame I was
> ever likely to meet, and I'd lost her because
> I'd acted like a horse's ass. And it turned
> out that way. I'd done something wrong
> and I had to pay for it, and so every time I
> fell in love again after that, I knew the dis-
> enchantment would ultimately turn up.
> And it did. Never failed. Because you get
> one chance at everything in life, and that's
> all.

There followed an interlude in Paris, where,
although he was too late for the golden age of
American expatriates peopled by F. Scott and
Zelda Fitzgerald, Ernest Hemingway, and Ger-
trude Stein, Huston would find the usual collection of almost-weres and might-have-beens, as
well as a number of talented people who would

make names for themselves as writers and artists in the years to come. Huston fit into this milieu as easily as he had fit into the New York and Hollywood scenes. He had ability as an artist, and for the year and a half that he stayed in Paris, he combined a serious immersion in art with a scraped-together existence in which he depended on the largesse of tourists to keep him alive.

Like many another artist before him, John parlayed charm and a gift of gab, together with a real facility for drawing, into meals and glasses of wine, purchased by bemused American tourists for whom this sort of encounter served as proof that they were experiencing the "real" Paris.

Huston's later art collections, which featured exceptionally fine pieces, probably owed their existence to his time in Paris, when he could absorb not only the works exhibited in the museums and galleries of the city, but the city itself. That period of his life affected at least one of his children strongly, too. Anjelica Huston comments frequently that her father insisted that people know what they were talking about and be able to qualify judgmental statements. Recalling the first time this affected her, she remembers a casual remark of hers at the family dinner table about Van Gogh that brought the full and not inconsiderable force of her father's attention on her. And then ensued a full-scale catechism as to why she held that opinion, what evidence she could marshal to defend it—questions an art history major, a Van Gogh devotee, or someone who had spent over a year on the streets of Paris could answer, but which she, at the time, could not.

Not everyone has John Huston's apparent ability to survive just about anywhere, no matter how many difficulties have to be overcome, and while surviving still take advantage of every experience encountered along the way. This sojourn in Paris, when prices were rising and no one had any money, when he had to survive on charm and native talent, might help explain Huston's later laissez-faire attitude toward Anjelica's years on her own after her mother's death. A man always in charge of his own life, Huston lacked the ability to see that others might not be so ready to assume full responsibility for themselves, and that being left to do it anyway could be viewed as neglect.

Huston kept himself alive in Paris and fed his soul from the splendid aesthetic banquet life in that great capital provided. When he returned to America, swallowing the pride that had kept him scrounging meals from tourists rather than accept money from relatives who had plenty of it, it was on a ticket Aunt Margaret bought. He sailed home seemingly no closer to knowing what he wanted to do with the rest of his life—or even the next six months of it—than he had been a year and a half before.

Others close to him seemed well on the road to fame. His father was rehearsing a dramatization of Sinclair Lewis's *Dodsworth* in New York, and William Wyler, a director John had met and worked with before he went to Europe, had a picture starring John Barrymore that was running well.

Acting might be the thing after all. He had gotten excellent notices on his very first try—and so, along with fifteen thousand men and women all over the country, John Huston took advantage of the Works Project Administration's Federal Theater, taking a job with one located in Chicago, and playing the title role in *Abe Lincoln in Illinois.*

Part of President Franklin D. Roosevelt's plan to provide work for the creative citizens of the nation while it suffered through the Depression, the Federal Theater, along with similar projects for writers and visual artists, pulled the arts into the mainstream of American life, exposing people to performances and exhibits who had probably never attended a play or gallery opening before, and introducing the artists involved in the various WPA projects to a different audience and a different perspective for their work.

This experience with out-of-the-ordinary theater audiences had a profound influence on John Huston's later work. As he said many years afterward, "I make movies for other people, not for myself." And movies, of course, are the medium of the masses, the nonelite.

What would have happened had an eighteen-year-old English girl not been visiting relatives and become part of the Chicago Federal Theater as a way to pass the summer can only be surmised. Huston's pattern of soaking up a person, a place, an experience, and then moving on, a pattern he repeated all his life, might have been repeated then, with the same somewhat aimless results he had had so far.

But Leslie Black, ten years younger than John, was in Chicago that summer of 1935, and although to John's dismay she did not immediately fall in love with him as he had instantly fallen in love with her, he couldn't blame her. In Leslie's eyes—and now in his own—John Huston was nobody, and nothing portended that the condition would soon change.

Nothing, that is, but John Huston's determination that the nobody Leslie met that summer would be somebody if and when she came back to Chicago the following year. Hollywood had had promise once, and he had been away long enough to believe that it could again. Leslie left for England; John headed west. Acting was put aside for the moment. Now he would write.

He found a job at Warner Brothers, stuck in a two-man office on the second floor of the writers' building, working for Jack and Harry Warner. Jack was hardly literate and didn't care who knew it. Harry had, if greater literacy, no more respect for writers than Jack did. John labored six days a week from nine until six, developing scripts with his office mate, Allen Rivkin, out of "buzz sessions" with other writers and fighting a system that wanted one cliché after the other, sprinkled liberally through formula stories that would produce the kind of pictures the Warners were certain American moviegoers wanted to see.

At no other time in his life would John Huston submit himself to such a rigorous schedule doing work for which he had little respect and less real interest. Visits to the movie set where William Wyler directed Walter Huston in the movie version of *Dodsworth* helped, as did the still-roaring

Hollywood party scene. John, tall, good-looking, with more than his share of Irish charm, was always welcome. He drank too much, he played around too much, he acted on impulses without regard to consequences—but he somehow stayed on the fine line that divides acceptably outrageous behavior from that which puts people beyond the pale.

Christmas Eve at the studio found John drunkenly reenacting a horse race for his audience of fellow writers and secretaries, riding the stair rail, exhorting his horse—having one hell of a time. Someone else had brought a .24 revolver to work, amusing himself by shooting out the light fixture that hung over the stairwell where John rode. Glass covered everything, including John's mount. Oblivious, John kept on—only to end the race with blood soaking through his jodhpurs. He had ripped out the seat of his pants and his shorts on the bits of shattered glass. A rescue team went off for a first-aid kit—when they returned, John had vanished. They finally found him giving the man with the gun a lesson in firing a deadly weapon—all delivered with drunken charm.

Perhaps a key to the almost universal acceptance John found among his peers, despite his boisterous behavior, is that he never blamed anyone else for what happened to him, took the consequences of his acts without complaint, and paid up when he had to. And so long as he played his games with people who could hold their own—the system worked. Where it broke down was when the people in the game weren't quite as tough or quite as smart or quite as independent. Dorothy Jeanne Harvey Huston was one of the first players sent to the showers after being unable to stand the roughness of the game, but she would not be the last.

For now, though, John balanced wild behavior with steady employment, perhaps releasing the frustration of such donkey work with his antics. Regular pay made his dream of marrying Leslie Black—a dream he had proposed to her within a quarter of an hour of meeting her—come true. In 1937, John and Leslie married. Many of the people close to John at the time said that marriage marked a turning point in his life. Henry Blanke, a Warner producer who believed in Huston's talent, and who had helped get him the job, was among those who believed that marrying Leslie was the best choice John had yet made. Though ten years younger than her thirty-one-year-old groom, Leslie apparently took "a drunken boy, hopelessly immature," as Blanke called him, someone whom Blanke considered "charming, very talented but without an ounce of discipline in his makeup," and brought out the abilities that would make the man.

In 1937 the Depression hung on in America, and in Europe the prospects for peace looked worse and worse. But for John Huston, the course he'd set when he married Leslie seemed to be heading very definitely in the right direction.

Artistically Huston had several assignments in a row that made solid blocks in the career he was building. His domestic life was going well, too. He and Leslie built a house near Tarzana from Huston's own design. He built the house on two knolls, putting a bridge between them that also served as a gallery to the structure. He offset the heat with a louvered attic that went the length of the house. Frank Lloyd Wright, the great American architect, came to see the house one day. He liked most of what Huston had done, but he did complain about the high ceilings, commenting that he himself liked the sense of shelter a low ceiling gives. When Huston explained that as a tall man he needed high ceilings, Wright replied that anyone over five-ten was a weed. The compliment Huston remembered most was when Wright said what a pleasure it was to see such natural expression from an amateur. Wright paid Huston another compliment, one delivered after the architect's death. If ever his life was filmed, Wright said, he wanted Huston to do it.

Over and over again throughout his life John Huston would win the acclaim of geniuses—still, no amount of approval ever seemed to make him forget the fact that his mother never gave him that gift. Rhea Huston Stephens died in 1938, and neither John nor Walter went to Seattle for her funeral. John, however, had been with her before she died. Rhea and her mother, the grandmother Huston called Gram, had been living in Los Angeles in an apartment, seeing a lot of John and his new wife, with whom they got along very well. This brief time before Rhea's last illness at least gave John Huston some good memories of the mother whose relationship with him had always been so complex.

Rhea developed headaches shortly after the move to Los Angeles. When they became more severe and more frequent, John called in a specialist, who said Rhea either had a brain tumor or was psychotic. The test to determine if she indeed had a tumor was rigorous, not to be taken lightly, and so Rhea went to a nursing home where she rapidly became much worse. Finally they had to make the test, which revealed a tumor on the brain.

By this time she could no longer speak. But when John sat with her just before the surgery and assured her that the doctor knew her problem and could fix it, she opened her eyes and said, "Can they fix it, John?" He assured her again that they could. Those were the last words either of them spoke to the other; Rhea went up to surgery, and he never saw her alive again.

Not long after Rhea's death, Walter and John worked together on Broadway—John directed his father in a play that won critical praise although it closed on March 16, 1940, after only four performances. But this was an honorable failure, because if the god of commerce had not been served by the play, the goddess of art was. John went back to Hollywood to work on a series of pictures that added luster to the already bright Huston name. While John concentrated on the scripts for *Sergeant York* and *High Sierra* and badgered Warners to give him a movie to direct, Leslie concentrated on having a baby. John reached his goal when Jack Warner gave him the go-ahead to make another version of *The Maltese Falcon*, the Dashiell Hammett novel that had already been made twice before. Leslie did get pregnant, but the baby was born prematurely. That death, John felt, ended their marriage, although they did not divorce until a couple of years later.

He recovered from the loss of the baby in a few weeks, but Leslie continued to grieve and found John uncaring. He should have been more understanding, he said many years later, or perhaps tried harder to see her through her grief. But with characteristic resilience Huston accepted the fact that they could not go back but must go ahead with their separate lives.

The separation may well have begun during the filming of *The Maltese Falcon*, not only the first film Huston directed, but one that became a classic. He, Mary Astor, Humphrey Bogart, Peter Lorre, and Sidney Greenstreet, who played the main characters in the film, had such a good time making the movie that when the day's shooting ended they repaired to the Lakeside Country Club, there to have a few drinks, eat supper, and talk until midnight. Such neglect of Leslie must have driven a wedge between them long before the baby's death.

But throughout his life John Huston paid more attention to the people involved in either his creative efforts or his favorite leisure activities—such as racing—than to people who happened to be connected to him by marriage or birth. Mary Astor was fun, Humphrey Bogart was fun—the whole wisecracking, joke-playing cast was fun, from the pranks they set up at the studio to shock visitors to the into-the-night conversations at the Lakeside Country Club.

Nor did John stop going out with other women. No one meeting John for the first time would have known he was married—he liked women, and they liked him, and the presence of a wife somewhere in the background didn't stop John from going out with women he met at Hollywood parties, nor, apparently, did the fact that he was married stop them.

Bogart gave Huston a nickname during the filming of *The Maltese Falcon*. He called him The Monster, and the name stuck. It seems peculiarly appropriate. Monsters are larger than life and are known for their habit of devouring people and things. Huston does not seem to have been a malicious monster—he was perfectly willing to accept blame when something didn't work out. He accepted the blame for the end of his marriage to Leslie, just as earlier he had accepted responsibility for the end of his marriage to Dorothy.

True, Dorothy chose to drink in response to Huston's affairs—and Leslie chose to let grief for the baby be the final wedge that split the marriage. On the other hand, the women attracted to men like Huston rarely have the strength or independent natures necessary to take charge of their own lives. The things friends laughed at and accepted—John's drinking and womanizing, his pranks and disregard of all conventions except the ones that suited him—would have sent strong women who could be happy in their own right fleeing into the night. John Huston did not attract women like that as wives and lovers, although he might have had them as friends.

Except for Evelyn Keyes, the tough little girl

from Atlanta who would be wife number three, Huston's wives seemed to the kind of women who allowed themselves to be swallowed up by him, who followed his lead without asking if the route led to a place that would be good for them, too. Had Leslie's baby lived, she would have had something to cling to—someone whose dependence on her would perhaps make up for the fact that John apparently needed her not at all. But the baby did not live, nor did the marriage.

But John the Monster, the eternal survivor, emerged from the ruins at the first breathtaking pinnacle of success. In early 1942, in his mid-thirties, with a world war beginning, John Huston's life promised all the new experiences and challenges even he could want.

An immediate parallel leaps into mind between John Huston and daughter Anjelica. John was in his mid-thirties before he really hit it big: daughter Anjelica was also in her mid-thirties before her film career, which had sputtered along with minor roles, took off and soared with *Prizzi's Honor*. It is interesting to speculate whether a longer "incubation" period for people of obvious talent results in a longer and ultimately more productive career. Certainly John Huston never stopped surprising people—as one reviewer of *The Dead*, the film starring Anjelica that Huston finished just before his death, wrote, "Who would have thought the old man had so much passion in him?"

And if John Huston had a string of accomplishments behind him at age thirty-five that his daughter Anjelica's modeling career and acting portfolio do not quite match, there is a difference between them that might account for the seemingly more productive years between adolescence and the mid-thirties the father seems to have had.

John Huston had a loving, highly supportive father, who from the time of his divorce from Rhea Gore Huston made sure he was a constant presence in his son's life. John Huston always knew that he had at least one parent in his corner, ready to open doors for him, ready to cheer him on.

And quite simply, Anjelica Huston did not. Her beloved mother could not help her, no matter how much love she had. The man who held the key turned it once—when Anjelica didn't come through for him, he waited a long, long time before he offered to turn it again.

As Peter Fonda said, contemplating his own difficult father, "Anjelica Huston was just as much out in the cold as I was."

CHAPTER 4

ONE of the reviewers of John Huston's autobiography, *An Open Book*, ended his review by commenting that although Huston showed "a master screenwriter's skill in setting a scene and delineating a character in a few words . . . he is content to remain on the surface of the events of his life. What is largely missing," the review concludes, "is the passion, insight, and conflict that inform his best films."

This reviewer did not understand the thing that set John Huston apart from other writers, other directors, other actors—indeed, set him apart from the greater percentage of the people he knew, loved, and worked with. This thing was not talent alone. There are many talented people in every field. It was not even the immensity of Huston's talent, as enormous as it was. Nor could his uniqueness be attributed to the diversity of his talent, his seeming ability to do anything he decided to do, and to do it well. Boxing, acting, painting, writing, directing—whatever field Huston entered, he performed well.

What, then, made him a legend? What gave him the capacity to have so many projects going on at the same time, each demanding enough to challenge the total talents of a lesser human being? Probably the very quality that the reviewer just cited saw as a lack.

Human beings of particular genius do not always use that genius well. One does not have to look further than Hollywood itself to see potentially great artists brought low by their own self-destructive behavior. All sorts of explanations can be given as to why one person of great talent manages to use it to the hilt and why another wastes it. But one reason might be found in the last two sentences of that review.

To people of less genius than John Huston, who could not sustain a life of such complexity as his always had for one week without giving way beneath the strain, much less carry it off for eighty-one years, his attitude toward his own life—another reviewer of the Huston book said Huston looked at his life as a cosmic joke—is the mark of a genius who not only survives the burdens that go with great talent, but survives with grace and style.

It is this very ability to stay on the surface of the events of life, to meet them as they come but then let them go, that allows certain creative geniuses to utilize their gifts and their lives fully, with little or no psychic energy wasted on spent passions and past conflicts. These people do not agonize over the past because they are too aware of the exigencies of the present, the possibilities of the future.

Men like Leonardo da Vinci, like Auguste Rodin, like Wolfgang Amadeus Mozart, whose music reveals nothing of his disordered life—these men, and John Huston can be counted among them, are blessed with both the genius to perceive reality with sensitivity and to then inform it with their own particular vision, and with the ability to put everything else in their lives into the perspective of that vision.

Because such people live at a deeper level of feeling than most other human beings, because their response to details both physical and subjective is more constant and more aware, they are actually able to process human experiences much more directly, and much more easily.

Their entire being is alive in the truest sense of the word, body, mind, and spirit all working together to absorb, respond, reflect, create—they simply do a better job of living fully than most humans do. And because of this heightened awareness, they see the possibilities of a situation much more rapidly than people who prefer to go through life blinded and deafened by their own defenses. Thus, when something occurs—a death, a reversal of fortunes—such genius-survivors, to coin a term, get past it much more quickly. They very often appear uncaring to those around them who are still slogging away in the Slough of Despond.

But—and this is an important element in the relationships such people have with others—men and women of that kind rarely understand at any level that really affects the way they respond to others that most people simply are not capable of living in this way.

Because people like John Huston take the consequences of their own choices, and usually make those choices for reasons that make sense to them regardless of what they look like to others, they do not understand that others don't make choices in that same way and are not prepared to take the consequences when the choices work out badly.

It was impossible that John Huston's later wives did not know that marriage never interfered with his relationships with other women. And yet they married him, and then led lives that apparently became impossible, since all of his marriages ended in unhappiness and divorce. One can almost imagine John Huston's wonder, if he thought about it at all, that after a woman had picked a bed to lie in from which her partner would frequently be absent, she allowed herself to become miserable when that proved to be the case.

One of the most difficult elements in the life of any genius is the lack of people who really understand the nature of the beast. Humphrey Bogart, a lifelong friend, coworker, and admirer of John Huston, must have been among the few who did understand the nature of this genius-beast: perhaps that is even why he affectionately termed him—The Monster.

In any case, the years between 1941 and 1946 were to demonstrate as perhaps nothing else could have John Huston's capacity to move into a new field and very soon command it. The diversity of his projects during these years, and the complexity of his relationships, make the war years almost a microcosm of a giant life, and the marriage that took place at the end of them showed as none of his others did his ability to keep to the surface of events rather than disturb the ongoing creative vitality beneath.

Just before Huston entered the U.S. Army as an officer in Special Services, he worked on a film called *In This Our Life*, starring Bette Davis with Olivia de Haviland in a supporting role. Huston fell in love with Olivia and proceeded to pay court to his new lady love with all the best camera shots. Jack Warner protested—after all, Davis was a much bigger star. But to no avail. Finally Warner used the best weapon on the set, Bette Davis herself. He showed Davis the film's rushes, with Huston and de Haviland sitting right there. When Davis finished exploding, John reshot the scenes under fire until both Warner and Davis were satisfied.

The conflict had no effect on Huston's relationship with Olivia, who agreed to marry him when he was free. Technically John and Leslie were still married, but he lived apart from her, and when Huston went to Washington later that year to be commissioned, it was "Livvy" who went with him.

Huston's first assignment was a documentary shot in the Aleutians; he next had an assignment in the States, before being sent overseas. Now a captain, he had fallen into the use of a Park Avenue apartment filled with fine paintings and stocked with vintage wines. During his stay in New York, Huston met the girl who would, years later, become his fourth wife. But when Tony Soma, a New York restaurant owner, introduced Huston to his thirteen-year-old daughter, Huston had not even met, much less married, wife number three.

Enrica Soma, at thirteen already showing the beauty she would possess when they met again, studied ballet. Huston invited her to go to the ballet with him, saying they would do it in grand style, riding in a hansom carriage—the whole nine yards. But when the night of their date arrived, Huston was flying across the Atlantic to London. Six years later, when they met at a dinner party at the David Selznicks', Enrica would remind Huston of that. "You stood me up on our very first date," she told him. He made up for that by taking her to bed with him that same night.

London in the fall of 1943 was a perfect setting for an adventurer like Huston. He took tailor-made shirts and uniforms from there to Italy, where he shot the second of the three documentaries he made in the Second World War. Battlefield filming was interspersed with crazy times like his reunion with Bogart in Naples, where Bogie was entertaining troops. Bogart and Huston joined the Rangers, the crack combat unit that always hit the beaches first, in a party just before the unit left for Anzio—the damage wreaked on both property and personnel surpassed even The Monster's finer moments, with young Rangers swinging from a chandelier suspended several stories above the hall's marble floor until it crashed to the ground, taking several of them with it, and breaking not a few bones and heads.

After Italy, Huston was ordered back to the States. He went to Hollywood to divorce Leslie and pick up his relationship with Olivia de Haviland, only to find her preoccupied with a suit against Warner Brothers, and too distracted to play. By the time he got his Las Vegas divorce, he and Livvy had drifted apart. She began dating someone else, and John, making the rounds of the Hollywood parties, added another chapter to his legend with a fight with Errol Flynn at a David Selznick party that put both combatants in the hospital.

The incident that started the fight between two men who hardly knew each other centered around a comment Flynn made about a woman for whom Huston still felt a great deal of affection, even though they no longer met. Huston took immediate issue, and he and Flynn left the party, going to a secluded spot at the bottom of the garden to fight it out. After more than an hour of fighting—"strictly according to Queensberry," Huston said—the combatants were discovered by guests leaving the party. They stopped the fight, which could be termed a draw, since both Flynn and Huston required overnight hospitalization. The fighters parted on good terms and would work on *The Roots of Heaven* in Africa some twelve years later.

Huston's chameleonlike ability to fit into any scene in which he happened to find himself made him attractive to the great, the near-great, and the never-would-be-great equally. During the war his rapport with his film crews and with the Italian people in the villages he filmed came from one part of his persona. At wild Hollywood parties another man emerged. And when Huston wanted to, he could hold his own with anyone.

On the heels of his divorce from Leslie and the erosion of his love affair with Livvy, Huston went to New York to film the last documentary he would do for the Army. It dealt with the psychological casualties of war: it was so powerful that the Army repressed it for almost thirty years before it finally had limited showings.

Huston had a casualty of his own in 1945, a love affair with a married woman named Marietta Fitzgerald. They met at the right—or wrong—psychological moment. Weary of war and violence, disappointed at the way his affair with Olivia de Haviland had worked out, Huston was ready to fall in love. And Marietta, daughter of an Episcopalian bishop and granddaughter of the founder of

Groton, though she was not at all the sort of woman to do such a thing, fell in love with him.

Married to a Wall Street attorney who served in the Army in the Far East, and mother of a five-year-old child, Marietta was, in Huston's words, "the most beautiful and desirable woman" he had ever known. She was also unhappily married and had in fact been on the point of separating from Desmond Fitzgerald when he received his commission and went off to war.

Huston would still dream about that summer in New York decades after the affair was only a treasured memory. It's easy to understand why. As Huston found, a city like New York changes in the summertime. It loses its hurried, harried, "big city" atmosphere and takes on a neighborhood ambience. Windows open and the life inside escapes into the streets. For lovers walking through such richness, New York became a magic place.

Once again Huston's happiness depended upon a divorce. With Olivia his marriage stood in the way. Now Marietta's did.

Walter Huston met Marietta and liked her very much, but he was not nearly so sanguine as his son that when Desmond came home and John and Marietta told him how they felt about each other, he would give Marietta a divorce. When Marietta left for her annual holiday with her parents at the end of the summer, Huston took up the slack with intense work on the new film at the mental hospital, and by occupying himself with a galaxy of friends when he came into New York.

A new friend, a woman Huston called "the

closest woman friend" he ever had, was Pauline Potter, who some nine years later would marry Baron Philippe de Rothschild. They met at a dinner party, and John offered to see Pauline home. It began to rain, and they took refuge in Jim Glennon's bar, one of John's favorite places to gather with close friends.

That was the beginning of their friendship; it would last all their lives. A cultured woman of good family but with little money, Pauline, according to Huston, was not really beautiful—but was still a great beauty. Her eyes, her walk, her voice, the way she brought out the best in the people talking with her—all of these things conspired to make her a unique and vastly attractive woman. Later, when she met the Baron de Rothschild, she made a comment that immediately won his heart. Introduced to one of the richest men in Europe, Pauline's response was to compliment him on his poetry, something much dearer to the Baron's heart than his money.

But then all sorts of things came to an end. In August the war was officially over, and Huston received his discharge. Desmond Fitzgerald came home and agreed to give Marietta a divorce—on one condition. She must first go through analysis. John protested that analysis could take years: Marietta promised that it would not. Not a year later, her analysis over, Marietta went through with the divorce. But by that time John Huston was married to somebody else.

And during those months John had to chafe under rules Marietta set. Although she called him, she would not allow him to call her, and not once did she say she loved him. Her restraint might have been part of her therapy, or the result of a promise made to Desmond—but whatever its cause, it proved frustrating for John. Frustration turned to despair as the months went by. For all he knew, the result of her analysis could be a renewed will to make her marriage to Desmond work.

Add to that frustration the predictable difficulty in returning to civilian life that all men and women coming home from war have, and it is easy to see why John Huston, on his return to Hollywood, soon earned a new nickname—Double Ugly. Commented a *Look* magazine writer, "He's a First Class character. . . . His uninhibited behavior pattern delights even hardened experts in the art of self-publicity. Not since John Barrymore has anybody handed the acting colony such outrageous subject matter for after-dinner conversations."

He showed perfect equality in the targets for his insults: no one was safe from them. He smeared Joan Crawford's rouge in full view of a room full of people with the comment that she wore too much makeup, and he turned up at an ultraformal Christmas Eve party hosted by ultraconservative hosts very late, very badly dressed, and very much the worse for wear after an evening of living-room wrestling matches with Bogart.

Such behavior might have become a full-time way of life for Huston, as it has for so many men who live out their lives in tolerant, always-ready-for-more-extravagant-tales Hollywood. But Huston, despite inner sorrow and outward disorder, was already involved in filming *The Treasure of the Sierra Madre*, a film that would be a bench mark in his already illustrious career and would gain for his father an Academy Award.

It was while working on the script for *Treasure* that John Huston met Evelyn Keyes. Despite a bad beginning with David Selznick, who had chased her around his office in an unsuccessful attempt to seduce her, Evelyn had been cast in Selznick's *Gone With the Wind* as Scarlett O'Hara's younger sister, and she was a guest at a Selznick dinner when Jennifer Jones, Selznick's wife, put John Huston next to her.

Described as a "pert, hazel-eyed blonde from a tough neighborhood in Atlanta," Evelyn apparently knew how to take care of herself. That quality may have been as appealing as any other to John Huston. His "biological need," as he called it, to fall in love when the war was over had been frustrated by the course of his affair with Marietta Fitzgerald. No one new had appeared on the scene—and when, after only knowing each other three weeks, Evelyn suggested that they get married, John, for reasons even he might have had difficulty sorting out, said yes.

Evelyn Keyes described the scene this way: "He remained hunched over the table . . . brows slightly raised, no smile, no flicker of—anything. He just looked at me for the longest time. And then he said—and I don't know what possessed *him*—'Why not?'"

Huston's recollection is essentially the same.

The whole affair had a made-up quality about it. They began the evening with dinner at Romanoff's, and by four the next morning, they were in Las Vegas getting married. Mike Romanoff provided the ring, one he'd found in his swimming pool, lost by some guest who never called about it. Huston chartered a plane to fly them to Vegas and back: the newlyweds were back at the Los Angeles airport at dawn, Evelyn to go to Columbia for work on *Johnny O'Clock,* and Huston to go to Warners.

Not until he was on his way back into town did "the utter damned absurdity" of the situation strike him. "How could I have done such a thing to Marietta? To Evelyn?" he asked himself. In fact, he thought about calling the whole thing off, but decided to stick with what he had done. There could be worse women for him than a pretty girl he described as "young and vivacious and companionable." There could be worse men for Evelyn than the man she found sure, authoritative—and fun—in bed. Huston told himself he had nothing to lose if he tried to make the marriage work. And Evelyn Keyes, standing on a lower rung of the Hollywood ladder looking up, must have thought that she hadn't, either. At any rate the deed was done, and when Pauline Potter, who'd heard the news on the radio, called later that day to ask if the report was true, and if John had a message for Marietta, he could give both questions a one-word answer. "Yes" to the first and "No" to the second.

David Selznick and Jennifer Jones threw what the *Hollywood Reporter* called a "spectacular shindig" in honor of the newlyweds, inviting "one hundred and fifty of his most intimate friends" to a party that lasted "until the sun came up over the mountains—and the band was still playing." James Stewart sang while Henry Fonda provided patter, Walter Huston sang his famous rendition of "September Song," and the fortune-teller, exhausted by "trying to tell famous and beautiful people how *much more* famous and beautiful they would become," collapsed by midnight.

A happy circumstance for the Hustons was that Humphrey Bogart, a man Huston considered one of his best friends, was also remarried after divorcing his first wife, whose drinking had become a horrendous problem. He married his leading lady in *To Have and Have Not*, a nineteen-year-old beauty professionally known as Lauren Bacall but called Betty by nearly everyone else.

Bogart's new marriage was taken seriously, but John's was not. The hasty wedding seemed to be just one more of Double Ugly's stunts, and even father Walter laughed at this latest trick.

With his personal situation set—at least for a while—Huston continued work on *Treasure*. Bogart would star in it, but first he had to make another film. The delay suited Huston, who had been asked to direct Jean-Paul Sartre's *No Exit* in New York. Evelyn accompanied John to New York. She had only known John's Hollywood persona. In New York she saw a man idolized by an entirely different set of friends, including Park Avenue society women with whom her husband seemed to have had—and to have—open-ended affairs. Women such as Marietta—now remarried herself—and Pauline Potter, now head designer at Hattie Carnegie, made even a girl who knew how to take care of herself feel inadequate.

Marriage to Huston was a constant parade of surprises. While on location in the wilds of Mexico for *Treasure*, Huston adopted one of the Mexican boys who ran errands for the company. Pablo was homeless and attached himself to Huston. There seemed no way to leave him behind, so when John flew home to Los Angeles, Evelyn found herself with a twelve-year-old son. Pablo would work on Huston's films in some capacity when he grew up, until he deserted his wife and three children to return to Mexico.

The Treasure of the Sierra Madre, winning Academy Awards for both Hustons, was a peak in John Huston's professional career. But if things were rosy at the studio, they were clouding up at home. The pet monkey that John carried around his neck became, along with the rest of his menagerie, the monkey on Evelyn's back. Allergic to animals, she found herself surrounded, not just by the horses and dogs John put on the ranch in the San Fernando Valley, but also by cats, parakeets, goats, monkeys, pigs, and even a burro called Socrates.

Had John kept his distance from the animals, or considered Evelyn's feelings, the menagerie might not have become such a bone of contention. But he did neither. Certain of the pets were with him constantly. A case in point is the chimpanzee Jennifer Jones gave Huston when they finished filming *We Were Strangers*. Named China after Jones's character in the movie, the chimpanzee was presented to Huston at the end-of-filming party.

By the time he left the party at three in the morning, it was too late to drive all the way out to the ranch. Evelyn had moved into town, into an elegant apartment in the Shoreham Apartments, and had had it decorated in white on white. When John arrived at the apartment, China in her cage, Evelyn was already asleep. "I couldn't bear to see China in a cage," John related. So he let her out.

Evelyn, awakened by the noise of China's "wonderful romp," came into the living room and immediately demanded that John do something about the chimp. Returned to her cage, China pushed the bars apart, rendering it useless. When John shut her into the bathroom, China screamed so loudly that John relented and took her out, telling Evelyn China would have to sleep with them that night. Fortunately for Evelyn, she had a refuge right upstairs, and she fled to it, staying the rest of the night with Paulette Goddard and Burgess Meredith.

Huston went to bed, taking China with him. "Clearly I had become her father, lover, and soul partner," he said, "and she had no intention of being separated from me."

What China did next might serve to substantiate the superior intelligence of chimps among the primates, because the destruction she wreaked on her rival's bedroom could not have been better calculated to make Evelyn fly into a rage. John heard her rampaging around during the rest of the night, and every time he called to her, she came back to bed and put her arms around him. But when he woke later that morning, he saw the havoc one small chimpanzee had been able to create in those excursions from his bed.

China had shattered Evelyn's glass counter that held her cosmetics and perfumes. All of those had been broken and spilled. China had ripped the curtains down and torn them to bits, and she had pulled open drawers, using them as well as every other surface in the room as a latrine. John lay in bed smoking, wondering what to do next, when Evelyn returned home. "Her reaction," he recalled, "was both predictable and understandable. She took one look, wailed, and slammed the door." Huston's was just as predictable. He saw no reason to punish an ape, and so he lit another cigarette.

Evelyn somehow rose to the occasion, even joining in Huston's laughter when the comic overtones of the scenario got too much for him. She even made overtures to China—who responded by biting Evelyn's hand to the bone, a wound that had to have highly painful cauterization.

That was the beginning—or middle—of the end of the Huston-Keyes marriage. The beginning of the end had probably been the day they married. Although Huston credited Evelyn with trying very hard to make the marriage work, she had any number of odds against her besides her allergies to animals. And most of the odds had women's names.

It would be a while before they divorced: Evelyn went with John to Key West to film *Key Largo*, which starred Humphrey Bogart and Lauren Bacall. John gambled the whole time they were there and lost heavily, recouping just before they returned home by betting the hotel manager five hundred dollars that his definition of the Immaculate Conception was not correct. A sleepy but cooperative priest confirmed that Huston was right—and Huston used the money he won to get back most of what he had lost.

Huston's gambling got him into trouble more than once, but it also got Evelyn into serious difficulties. They were back in Hollywood shooting *Key Largo* when Huston entered a horse he owned in a six-furlong race at the Santa Anita track. He had reason to believe that the horse, a long shot, would come in first, and he gave Evelyn every dollar he could lay his hands on to bet. She should spread the money around, John instructed, so that no one would see her betting on Lady Bruce.

Lady Bruce did win, and in one marvelous moment Huston went from a debt-ridden existence to the carefree, expansive—and expensive— lifestyle he lived whether he could afford it or not. A lot of friends and *Largo* crew members had also bet on Lady Bruce, and Huston planned a jubilant celebration at Chasen's restaurant for that night.

Shortly after the race ended, a friend of Huston's called him to tell him the bad—and unbelievable—news. Evelyn had not bet the money on Lady Bruce. She had run into another horse's owner and trainer, who had convinced her that their horse would win. She put one hundred dollars on Lady Bruce, and all the rest of the money on another horse.

Evelyn felt terrible, the friend said, and was afraid to face John or even talk to him on the phone. Huston stuggled against his shock, disappointment, and anger and told the man to tell Evelyn it was okay, to come on.

He went to Chasen's to wait for Evelyn, who didn't show up. Finally she called to say she just couldn't face him. Huston maintained his gentleman's role for a while, telling her over and over to forget it, to come on and meet him, that it was only money. Evelyn kept protesting, trying to explain why she believed the other men rather than him. That proved to be the last straw. "You bitch!" Huston roared. "You dismal, wretched, silly bitch!" By the time she got to Chasen's, Huston was too drunk to even recognize her.

Such vignettes contain the seed of an entire story. The iconoclastic hero, risking all on one race. The woman he sends to do his bidding, who inexplicably listens to men other than himself! The inevitable loss. And then the particular epithets used to describe the woman's behavior. Not stubborn. Not arrogant. Not even spiteful. Dismal. Wretched. Silly. Bitch. If Evelyn Keyes didn't know then what Huston thought of her, she was sillier even than he thought.

Or perhaps the peculiar fascination monsters have kept her married to Huston long after common sense should have told her to get out. It was not as though the little tough girl from Atlanta did not know how to take care of herself. When the divorce did come, Evelyn's lawyer took John to the cleaners. She ended up with all his cash, their jointly owned real estate, all the paintings, and half of his pre-Columbian art collection. She would later get the rest of it when Huston ran into her in Paris a year or so after the divorce and offered to flip a coin to see who would give the other the rest of the collection so it would all be under one roof. The gods were laughing at Gambling John that day. Evelyn won.

Huston shot *The Asphalt Jungle* after *Key Largo,* pulling out of newcomer Marilyn Monroe a performance that made her boss, Darryl F. Zanuck, say: "Jesus, she was good in it. . . . It must have been the magic of Huston because I didn't think she had all that in her."

By early 1950 major changes were occurring in John Huston's life. His marriage to Evelyn Keyes came to an official end in Juárez, Mexico, on February 10, 1950. It had of course been in a slow stall for a long time. Now its end was precipitated by another encounter with Enrica Soma, the daughter of Tony Soma whom Huston had met six years before in New York, and who now, at age nineteen, was a George Balanchine ballerina, a *Life* magazine cover girl, a contract player for David O. Selznick—and a guest at a dinner party at the Selznicks', where once again John Huston found himself seated next to a woman who would become his wife.

This time there was a vignette from the past— a hook for their story—to establish instant rapport. Huston described Enrica as a "modern Mona Lisa."

But when Ricki teased John, saying he had once failed to keep a date with her, and reminding him of that long-ago time when he had promised her a romantic carriage ride to see the ballet, the whole matter was undoubtedly settled then and there. A man much less imaginative and sexually restless than Huston would have been intrigued by the situation: here was a girl he met when she was thirteen, whom he had made a date with, and then broken when the war called him away, all grown up, and in the words of Evelyn Keyes, at a "fuckable age."

Ricki Soma was certainly not the first woman—or probably even "girl-child," as Evelyn called her—that Huston had slept with during his marriage to Evelyn, but she was the first one, apparently, to have an irate Italian father in the background threatening lawsuits and calling Huston a "reckless libertine." Or maybe Ricki was just the first one to get pregnant. And whether the liaison resulted because, as Evelyn charged, Enrica had no reluctance about using her "newfound wiles," or whether, as her outraged parents believed, the forty-three-year-old Huston had seduced their daughter, using his own time-tested wiles, the result was the same. Enrica was going to have Huston's child, and he had to make it legitimate.

He did make it legal—if, that is, California courts accepted the Mexican divorce—on February 11, 1950, the day after his quick trip to Juárez.

Tony Soma, Ricki's father, said of Huston that "he is a mystery to himself, and he doesn't want to be analyzed." However, since Ricki went to the house at Tarzana with Huston the night she met him at the Selznicks', there seems little mystery to this particular tale. There could have been no possible doubt in her mind as to the outcome of the evening: a boy her age might have slept in another bed, but a man Huston's certainly wouldn't.

If there is any mystery, it is in why Huston took so long to divorce Evelyn and marry Ricki. Certainly when Evelyn moved into town and he stayed out at the Valley ranch or at the Tarzana house, the Keyes-Huston marriage was all over. And while the truth would have come out at any point, waiting until Ricki was seven months pregnant to marry her seems a little strange even for the flamboyant Huston.

Perhaps he didn't really believe Ricki was pregnant. Perhaps he thought the child had been fathered by someone else. Perhaps he thought it would all blow over, and that the Somas would stop yelling and he wouldn't have to do anything at all. It's an odd scenario, a man of Huston's experience being caught by the oldest ploy of all. By the time he and Ricki married, he had had relationships with dozens of women—but so far, he had not fathered a child. Or if he had, none had claimed him as the father.

It is interesting, too, to speculate about the arrival of another baby some fifteen months after Walter Anthony Huston arrived on April 16, 1950, just ten days after his grandfather's death. Perhaps Ricki wanted another baby to rear with her son. Perhaps Huston wanted to show the world—which must have been a little agog at this latest Huston caper, no matter how inured it thought it had become to Double Ugly's tricks—that his fatherhood had been no accident, and to prove it—here—he'd do it again.

At any rate, in July of 1951, a telegram arrived for John Huston, at the time deep in the Belgian Congo filming *The African Queen*. Katharine Hepburn, starring with Humphrey Bogart in the film, recalled that Huston read the message, then stuck it in his pocket without saying a word.

"For heaven's sake, John, tell us!" Hepburn cried.

"It's a girl," Huston replied.

And so the next Huston star, Anjelica, was born.

CHAPTER 5

*A*NJELICA arrived at a propitious time in her father's life. *The African Queen* was produced by Horizon Pictures, a venture owned by Huston and Sam Spiegel. An artistic and commercial success, the picture would become yet another Huston classic, one that still draws devoted fans when it plays on television. Humphrey Bogart seemed a logical choice to play Charlie Alnutt, the mailboat captain whose boat carried the unlikely duo on their incredible voyage. Katharine Hepburn did not seem as likely a choice for Rosie Sayer, the missionary lady who must willy-nilly trust herself to Charlie when her brother dies.

It is interesting to note that this great lady of film was left untouched by Huston's fabled charm when they first met. "That studied old-Kentucky-colonel charm," she called it, saying that "Frankly, I think he's one of the overmasculine boys who fascinate themselves and the New York critics being great guys . . ."

And in the beginning of filming, Bogart wasn't all that impressed with his leading lady, either. "She won't let anybody get a word in sideways," he told the *Hollywood Reporter*. "At first I felt as though I was expected to kiss the hem of her skirt, or to lie down on my face in the dirt before her." But as weeks in difficult locations went by, Bogart's attitude toward Katie Hepburn changed.

"In the jungle I always griped. . . . But Kate was in heaven. She couldn't pass a tree, or a bush, without wanting to know its precise origin." By the time filming was over, Bogart was squarely in Hepburn's camp. "When we finally left Africa, she made the rest of us feel like tired old men. She rented a bicycle at Shannon Airport, during our six-hour layover, and peddled all over the Irish countryside. Kate's quite a gal!"

And by this time, Katharine Hepburn thought John Huston was quite a guy. She couldn't quite get a handle on Rosie until Huston came over to her on the second day of shooting and said that Rosie is "almost always facing what is for her a serious situation" and is "a pretty serious-minded lady," then asking her if she had ever seen "you know—newsreels—of Mrs. Roosevelt—those newsreels where she visited the soldiers in the hospitals?" Assured that she had, Huston went on, "Do you remember, Katie dear, that lovely smile. . . ?"

Think of that smile, he told her. "Like Mrs. Roosevelt—she felt she was ugly—she thought she looked better smiling—so she . . . The society smile."

And having planted the seed, he left her to think it over. And she did. And came to the conclusion that she had just heard the "goddamnedest best piece of direction" anyone had ever given her. "And he's just told me exactly how to play this part. . . . Such fun. I was his from there on in."

Once again Huston's real genius more than made up for any earlier impression he might have made. By the end of filming, Hepburn had gone elephant hunting with Huston, getting entirely into the spirit of being in a wild location with one of Hollywood's wildest men. Lauren Bacall, who was along to be with her husband, wrote in her autobiography that the contrast between the essential natures of Bogart and Huston really came to the fore in this film. "John really became a white hunter in Africa—he believed he *was* one— and he adored it; he didn't care how long he stayed. That was John. Bogie was different—he wanted to be back in civilization. He had a life he'd built, nurtured, cared about . . . John was fantasy—Bogie reality."

These are interesting comments, particularly the one stating that Huston didn't care how long he stayed. John and Enrica had been married only about a year and a half at the time—and his new baby girl had just arrived back in Malibu.

The filming of *The African Queen* throws into sharp relief Huston's propensity for creating realities that would then enable him to get what he wanted. He put his cast into horrendous conditions—and got the performances of their lives. Now he had two children—a family. The decision he made to bring them up in a reality so different from the one he himself had known is understandable—as he himself said, having never had a stable home, he wanted to make sure his children had one.

And yet when he found that home for them, it was not even in the land of their birth. As though he were deliberately separating them from all the events and people and creative forces that might have made them understand what kind of man their father was, he would settle Ricki and the children in Ireland, where he created for them a replica of a life already dying, imbuing them with traditions that did not work even for the Irish natives very well.

Or maybe Huston believed that a return to his own Irish roots would be just what he needed to make him change his ways. At any rate, he had a love affair with Ireland, one that first began when he attended the Galway Blazer Hunt Ball at the Gresham Hotel in Dublin shortly before he went to Africa to begin work on *The African Queen* and only a few months before Anjelica was born.

The ball was reminiscent of the Ranger party in Naples during the war, when daring young men had leaped from the balcony of the great hotel in which they were housed. The hunt ball ended the same way, with young Irish bucks jumping off a balcony above the dance floor. "His followers came after him, one after another," Huston said, "until the floor was littered with young men with broken bones and heads." For Double Ugly, such men must have made him feel very much at home.

His invitation to the ball had come from Lady Oonagh Oranmore and Browne, one of three sisters whom Huston called "witches . . . capable of changing swinish folk into real swine before your very eyes, and turning them back again without their even knowing it." Lady Oranmore and Browne and her sisters were also beautiful, and when Huston went to her place in County Wicklow, and was exposed to the Irish way of life—at least the way of life as Oonagh lived it—that, combined with the spectacular scenery, made him, in his words, "Ireland's own."

It would be a while before Huston returned to Ireland with his family: in the meantime there would be two other pictures, *Moulin Rouge*, shot in Paris, and *Beat the Devil*, with Italian locations. The first made a lot of money, and the second, at first a disaster, became a cult classic years later— it still holds that distinction.

Ricki, with Tony and baby Anjelica, met John in Paris, where he first saw his new daughter. Huston rented a château in Chantilly and settled his family into it while work went forward on *Moulin Rouge*.

The addition of another child to his list of dependents and the expense of maintaining his family abroad apparently had no effect on Huston's devotion to the track. Not only did he bet extensively on French horses, but he got his friend Billy Pearson, a jockey whose relationship with Huston went back many years, to come to Paris to ride a horse Huston bought. The venture was not successful, and Huston continued to lose money he could ill afford to lose. Despite the commercial success of *The African Queen*, Huston realized very little from it. "It was one of the most successful pictures I ever made," he said later. "And Sam got all the money."

One bright spot in the Hustons' financial darkness was a race John won in London, betting 30–1 odds on a horse named Thunderhead II. He had put an immense amount of money on the race—money he didn't have. Lady Luck not only smiled on Huston that day, she hugged and kissed him. The horse ran home more than eight lengths out front, and Huston won a bet of several thousand pounds paying 30 to 1.

The Hustons were definitely in the money now—and according to the law at that time, all but ten pounds of it had to be spent in England. Enrica came over from Paris and bought out the stores—she bought clothing and gifts for the children, John bought bronzes and objects of art.

Moulin Rouge was lucky, too. It made money, money that would allow John Huston to take the first step toward living in Ireland, that of renting a house called Courtown in County Kildare.

Anjelica Huston recalled the various threads

that twisted together and made up her father's decision to move to Ireland. "He loved hunting," she said, "[and] he was disillusioned with America, with McCarthyism; his work was taking him to Europe." Commenting that the nature of her father's life was to incorporate every country attached to one of his movies, she said he fell in love with Europe while making *Moulin Rouge.*

From there his progression to Ireland seemed natural. "He's always loved wild places, and Ireland was nothing if not wild. . . . He decided it would be a great place for my brother and me to grow up, and so he bought a house there."

The house he bought, St. Clerans, was near Galway City in the western coastal region of Ireland. Huston first saw it while hunting from Courtown, the rented house where he lived with Ricki and the children. Then a few months later Ricki saw the same house while visiting friends. Now vacant and for sale, its architecture—that of a Georgian manor house—sold it to John. The house sat on an estate of 100 Irish acres (the equivalent of 110 in the U.S.) and had all sorts of gardens, ranging from a vegetable garden to one filled with examples of exotic trees from all the world, grown from seedlings Irish sea captains had brought back home.

Here was the site of the "castle and the gatehouse" Anjelica remembered from her childhood years. St. Clerans had the manor house in the front, and then, across a trout stream, a thirteenth-century tower (the same century, incidentally, to which John Huston's family could be traced) and other outbuildings, including stables, quarters for the groom, and the steward's cottage. They redid the cottage-like gatehouse first, and even after the manor had been completed in all its splendor, Ricki preferred the little house.

That little house must have seemed like a wonderful refuge to twenty-year-old Ricki, who had grown up under the shadow of a man almost as much of a showman in his field as John Huston was in his. "My grandfather was a yogi," Anjelica said. "He would stand on his head every day reading Shaw and Voltaire and saying the most fantastic things, like, 'The tongue is the root of all life.'"

Tony Soma owned Tony's and Tony's Wife, the equivalents of the time of today's Elaine's restaurant in New York City. Ricki saw celebrities every day and heard her father give famous people unconventional advice. "Always sing with your teeth clenched" was Soma's advice to Frank Sinatra, and he insisted that Ricki write a two-page essay on every ballet she saw.

No wonder she enjoyed having her own terrain, a place she could make beautiful in her own way. Anjelica remembers a mother who "loved beautiful things—fresh-cut flowers, tiny boxes with hidden compartments, potpourris, and the Balenciaga dresses" she watched her beautiful mother wear. Anjelica still owns a perfect copy of the 1947 *Life* magazine that put her mother, photographed by Philippe Halsman, on the cover. People who have seen that cover comment on the similarity between the two faces—the "same dark

Mona Lisa gaze . . . with eyebrows shaped like cockeyed parentheses."

Ricki and Anjelica Huston shared beauty in that cottage on the great Irish estate, beauty remembered in the treasured mementos of Anjelica's childhood, including the Renaissance angel that used to watch over her bed, that are kept safe in Anjelica's present home.

While Ricki and the children settled into quiet domesticity, John Huston blew in and out of the scene, going off on this film or that, coming back with things for St. Clerans he collected from all over the world. The house must have been fantastic. John sent an entire bath over from Japan, one that could hold up to six bathers, and that was, as he commented, "wonderful after hunting." The bath had shoji doors and mats; other Oriental influences were found in the dining room, where the wallpaper was made of reproductions of the print John saw on a Kenzo screen in Japan, and in the drawing room, where an ancient Chinese design had been woven into the silk curtains especially for him.

A three-storied house with a moat around the lower floor—the entrance was on the second floor—the place was enormous, and by the time Huston had finished with it, it must have seemed more like a movie set than a home. The main hall was paved with marble, and the rooms were filled with Chinese porcelain, paintings by Juan Gris and Morris Graves, ceramics dating from the Etruscan period forward, a Japanese "fan painting" collection, African bronzes and fabrics, antiques from England and France, Mexican tiles in the kitchen and all bathrooms, a thirteen-foot Georgian dining-room table with matching chairs, a Louis XV drawing room, Egyptian pieces, and one of Monet's famed "Water Lily" paintings. Eclectic and daring—a decor only a man like John Huston would dream of doing without the advice of a professional—or of his wife.

Huston's bedroom had, as he described it, "a big, canopied, four-poster Florentine matrimonial bed, carved with doves and flowers." It also had two Louis XIV chairs, a chest that had originally stored vestments in a French church, and a thirteenth-century Greek icon. All the bedrooms and all the baths had fireplaces.

John Huston did not share that magnificent bed with Ricki: at least, Anjelica doesn't remember her parents ever sharing a bedroom. "I think I never asked my father anything because I was so afraid he would tell me the answer," she said.

She does remember going to her father's room at ten o'clock on the mornings he was at home. He sat up in bed holding court, with Tony and Anjelica curled up near him, drawing pictures and talking. "We were happy for his just being there," Anjelica said. But she believes that her father took more to what was adult in children than to what was childish. Because of her father's intelligence, Anjelica said, he didn't suffer fools gladly. "You didn't want to get on his wrong side."

Anjelica remembers her mother as being a woman who possessed not only style and beauty, but great taste and a sharp wit. Growing up with a young and devoted mother made her father's absences much less important. "We never felt half-orphaned," Anjelica said. While Huston's appearances were erratic and overwhelming, day-to-day life with Ricki Soma was an exploration, a constant exposure to what Anjelica loosely terms "culture." "She was always telling Tony and me to ask questions, to wonder about the what and why."

Anjelica went to the local convent school, taught by Irish nuns. The choice of schools had more to do with convenience—the Hustons would otherwise have had to send Anjelica to boarding school—than it did with any desire for religious training on her parents' part. Neither parent was religious: Anjelica wasn't forced to take catechism or to learn thc Bible. The main memory she has of those convent schooldays is the beauty of the nuns. At that time, in the late fifties, nuns still wore habits, and Anjelica found their attire, black from head to toe, with flowing veils, quite romantic. Like many little girls enamored of nuns, she thought for a while that she wanted to be one. When she confided this desire to her father one day when he was driving her home from school, he told her he thought this a splendid idea, and when did she want to begin?

Anjelica abandoned the idea of becoming a nun but kept her penchant for veils. When she and close friend Joan Buck played "dress-up," a game they never tired of, Joan's costumes were always plum colored and Anjelica always had a veil.

Joan was the daughter of Jules and Joyce Buck, both close friends of John Huston. (He and Jules had worked together during World War II.) The Bucks came to St. Clerans the Christmas Anjelica was six and Joan was nine. Recalling that meeting, Anjelica said she could remember every detail perfectly. "Joan was pale and dark, with shoulder-length hair." Joan carried a green leather handbag with a big brass decoration in one hand and a stack of Little Lulu funny books in the other. That was the beginning of a friendship that lasted until they were both in their twenties. Then, after a period of estrangement Joan Buck later referred to as "classic English novel material," they renewed their closeness.

As adults, both Anjelica and Joan would shine in the creative arts. Joan's second novel, *Daughter of the Swan,* was published to critical acclaim the same year Anjelica won her Oscar. But at St. Clerans the imaginations that would later produce Maerose Prizzi and Buck's novels found their outlet in playing dress-up.

John Huston recalled a Christmas Eve when the man who usually played Santa Claus at the traditional party for the Huston staff and neighboring farm families was ill and couldn't come. Author John Steinbeck and his wife Elaine were among the houseguests that year, and after much persuasion, Steinbeck gave in and said he would be Santa Claus.

"He docilely accepted the ministrations of Anjelica and her friend Joan Buck as they adjusted his raiment and stuck on his white beard and eyebrows with spirit gum," Huston remembered.

Joan often took the lead in the festivities, being older and more of an extrovert than the younger Anjelica, whom she remembers as being "small and complicated and shy." That very first Christmas, Joan decided that the children would do a play to be presented to the adults. "Halfway through the opening speech," she recalled, "Anjelica stopped, looked up, and announced: 'I don't like it and I won't do it.'" An early indication of the will that would later help Anjelica emerge from living in the shadow of a famous father and an equally famous lover into a spotlight of her own.

All the Hustons remember those Christmases at St. Clerans as wonderful occasions, with rituals established and followed every year. Christmas officially began on December 20th when a tree that stood in the main hall and rose up two floors through the stairwell was carried in and decorated.

The staff and neighbors' party on Christmas Eve featured a toast and three cheers for the "Squire"—John Huston—followed by food, drink, songs, poems, dancing, and tales such as only the Irish can tell. Many years later, when St. Clerans was but a treasured memory, John Huston would star daughter Anjelica in *The Dead*, a story by James Joyce that recaptures exactly that sort of holiday spirit.

"The best years of my life," John Huston would say about the years at St. Clerans, and the children agree, calling their childhood an idyllic time. Few American children have the kind of

Christmas memories Anjelica and Tony have, no matter how luxuriously they were reared.

The family and houseguests gathered on Christmas morning between ten and eleven o'clock, drinking champagne as they opened their gifts. Since John might have been halfway around the world since he had last been home, the gifts he brought were both exotic and extravagant. After an hour or so, friends from the country arrived, people Huston had met with the Galway Hunt. More champagne, more gifts—and then dinner at three o'clock, with never less than fourteen at table.

That table came straight out of a grand and glorious dream, with old Waterford crystal, heavy Georgian silver, flowers from Ricki's hothouse, gleaming Irish damask, and all the traditional foods. A life of splendor and privilege that extended into so mundane a thing as school. Anjelica says she always received special consideration at the convent because the nuns held her father in such awe.

As did the local people. Huston was even asked to be Joint Master of the Hunt, an honor that depended to some degree on his ability to help finance its activities, but it would never have been conferred on a mere rich American if he had not been the kind of man the Irish adored. A mutual love affair between a man and a lifestyle he helped create—with his young children growing up in a fairy tale he must have known he could not maintain.

Huston himself called life at St. Clerans "as

beautiful and fantastic as a masquerade," recalling dinners lit by fifty candles whose light gleamed off women in formal gowns and men in black ties. A dying tradition by the time Huston moved himself and his family to Ireland—but one that creative imagination and money managed to keep up for the first decade of Anjelica's life.

Joan Buck remembers being sent to Ireland during the holidays to have a "normal life," one that had "children and dogs." But she saw it as magical, not normal. "There were Anjelica and her brother Tony. There were horses and the Irish countryside." Buck adored Ricki, to whom she dedicated her novel *Daughter of the Swan*. The Irish mysticism entered her soul: she believes it entered Anjelica's, too.

"It was a magical childhood that abides. The Irish songs and the bits of Yeats and the passionate Irish nationalism remain as backgrounds, I think, for both of us," she said.

It was also an isolated childhood. Anjelica Huston told an interviewer that growing up in Ireland gave her a different set of idols than those of more typical American teenagers. "One's cultural heroes were not necessarily famous, or famous in that they were faces . . . seen on television or in the movies." They lived in a very remote part of Ireland: Anjelica saw only her father's movies, shown in the projecting room at St. Clerans, until she moved to London with her mother at age ten.

If Ricki was the constant star on whom Anjelica and Tony could set their compasses, John was the comet that streaked brilliantly through their sky.

"He would descend like Santa Claus, bearing extravagant gifts, and lead us in a few weeks of hectic play before evaporating again," Tony Huston said. "Between the fox hunting, trips to the bogs of Connemara, evenings in oyster bars, visits to Japanese baths, and dress-up nights, he'd make attempts at instant fatherhood that usually ended badly," he added.

Adolescence was a particularly hard time. The friends and coworkers and hangers-on that always accompanied Huston to St. Clerans, or arrived like swallows returning to Capistrano whenever word got out that he was there, supported him even when he levied the most devastating criticism at his children. "It became a spectator sport to see who would be taken apart next, who would rush out of the room in tears," Tony said.

Joan Buck tracked Anjelica's growing up, saying that when they were children, Anjelica was braver about horses than Joan and could almost speak Gaelic. Anjelica kept on being braver than Joan when they hit adolescence—"braver about dancing and boys; I was better at French."

And looking back on the one friendship—the one person outside her immediate family, it seems, whose relationship with Anjelica goes back to that magical time—Anjelica sounds like any other girl recalling any other friendship.

"We became inseparable. We spent long summers growing up, taking day trips out to the cliffs of Moher, where we'd see schools of porpoises, or to Connemara to investigate ancient graveyards and climb Martello Towers." She remembers picnics and pony rides, dog shows and spontaneous plays. Learning the twist and talking about boys. Living with the Bucks in London while Ricki found a place for herself and her children to live when her marriage to John hit the rocks. Joan's coming to see Anjelica at recess during the first awful weeks at the new London school.

Some observers note Anjelica's capacity to "float above her catastrophes, untouched by a proper formal education, unresponsive to certain internal questions." This capacity might have been inherited from her father—or developed almost as if by osmosis, so like is it to Huston's capacity to surmount the most tumultuous crises and still retain the ability to focus on his work.

Although father and daughter had quite different childhoods, there might be a thread of emotional similarity. John's parents divorced when he was three, and he lived a very unstable life in terms of place, moving with his mother as he grew up, then swinging back and forth between parents later. Still, Walter Huston provided an emotional stability that gave his son an inner "place," a base of security from which he could operate.

Anjelica had stability of place—more so than most people of her generation, for in that remote spot in Ireland, the influences of popular culture were totally ineffective. St. Clerans was a bulwark against change: life was ritualistic, life was beautiful, life was untouched by the twentieth century. Like a princess in a fairy tale, Anjelica lived hidden away. And she had her mother, whose constant presence and love gave her that inner "place," too.

But princesses in fairy tales are supposed to be discovered by the prince who will marry them and with whom they will live happily ever after, going from their father's castle to an equally splendid one of their own. Anjelica Huston's childhood sounds like a preparation for just that kind of life. Certainly, although she was exposed to all sorts of famous people, and although when she moved to London she was taken to plays and museums by her mother, Anjelica's education seems to have been catch-as-catch-can. Neither parent, of course, had formal education in terms of university degrees, and although John Huston does not seem to have said anything on the subject, he probably would have scoffed at the idea that any child of his would benefit by exposure to academia. Still, there are strong arguments to be made for allowing even children of such iconoclasts as John Huston to test themselves in the traditional way. Much is discovered about oneself in a university setting—and a great many of the discoveries have to do with learning that there are more ways than one to live and to think.

Such knowledge can help its owner withstand blows when they inevitably come. Without it, the discoveries will still have to be made—but they often come through following a harder and crueler road.

Anjelica Huston did not leave her father's remote castle to go live in one of her own. In 1961,

Ricki took Anjelica and moved to London. Tony remained at St. Clerans. Commenting on her mother's life, Anjelica said, "My mother's life in Ireland must have been quite repressive. My father was usually away, working. For his part, my father always had a taste for adventure, a taste for the good things. That included other women. Eventually my father had a son with another woman, and my mother had a daughter with another man. It was evident that things were never going to go back to where they had been."

Nor did they. Although the Hustons did not divorce, and although the family still gathered at St. Clerans for Christmas and holidays, the curtain had finally dropped on a long, enchanted first act. The spell had been broken now, and when the curtain went up on the next act in Anjelica's life, it found her living in London with her mother. They lived first in an apartment near Regent's Park, and later in an Edwardian house in the St. John's Wood part of London, a neighborhood called Little Venice.

In the way life has of repeating itself, John had made someone else pregnant, Zoe Sallis, an Anglo-Iranian girl who would later appear in both *Night of the Iguana* and *The Bible*, and who, in 1962, presented John with his second son, Danny.

John's marriage to Evelyn Keyes had ended with a bang when he bolted to Juárez, got a Mexican divorce one day, and married Ricki back in California the next. His marriage to Ricki never really ended in legal terms—at the time of her death in 1969 they were separated, but not divorced. It just went into a long, slow, fade, with occasional reappearances by the roving husband and father.

In 1964, Huston became an Irish citizen, saying at the time that he wanted to get back to the roots of his ancestors. The tax advantages of no longer calling the United States home couldn't be overlooked, either. Huston and the Irish had an affinity for each other. He always thought that they had treated him particularly well when they learned that this hard-riding, hard-drinking, generous man didn't believe in God. In Catholic Ireland, to be an atheist is tantamount to admitting that one's eternal destination is hell. "They tried to make things pleasant for me—temporarily," Huston said. His children also became Irish citizens.

There was little change in Anjelica's relationship with her father once she and Ricki moved to London: she had never seen much of him, and now she saw him no less. Huston often told people how devoted he was to marriage and family, proclaiming that he made all these movies for the benefit of his family as much as for himself. The fact that those movies took him away from them didn't seem to impinge on his consciousness at all. Moviemaking was his kingdom, as Anjelica termed it. "He's a Leo . . . so he has a kingdom, and he was trying to keep his kingdom there."

Much later, when Tony's first child was born, and Huston was reflecting over his past life as he wrote his autobiography, he would say that if he had it all to do over again, there were five things he would change. First on that list is—"I would spend more time with my children."

How sad that the realization came too late to make up for all those years in which, as Anjelica remembers, "he was too busy caring for a whole lot of things that he couldn't get to us except for one week in a year."

CHAPTER 6

ANJELICA at ten was slender,
dark, delicate. She looked like her mother, as did
Tony. For a time Anjelica returned to Ireland, to
board at the convent where she had been a day
student. As a teenager she would live in London
and attend the French lycée there, a place where
she experienced complete misery. Her rural Irish
schooling had hardly prepared her to compete
with students so much better grounded than she.
And while no one had verbalized goals for her,
there seemed to be some sort of family agreement
that Anjelica would be an actress. To a girl with
that vague destiny, the focused study of school-

mates headed for prestigious universities must have seemed a strange way to spend time. At any rate, Anjelica's attendance at the lycée was sporadic at best. An imaginative girl, she found ample excuses for not going to school.

The normal problems of adolescence were complicated by the fact that their living standard in London didn't come up to the expansive, expensive lifestyle Anjelica had been reared with. She remembers that the change from being very spoiled as a child to an adolescence marked by the lack of things she had always taken for granted had a bad effect on her. "I was embarrassed when the subject of money was brought up," she said. "It was humiliating to me, which must have been pretty horrible for my poor mother."

Anjelica reacted to pain the way so many adolescents do: she let her hair grow long, wore the white makeup so popular in the Sixties, piled on the eye makeup—and of course smoked at school. All this may have been cool in London, but when she visited her father in Ireland, he was appalled. An interesting reaction from a man who did exactly as he pleased all of his life, and who earned the nickname Double Ugly in Hollywood because of his outrageous pranks! But perhaps John Huston saw the difference between his own behavior, which was part and parcel of the way he always lived, and Anjelica's behavior. Hers was, after all, the uniform rebellion. His was Life on the grand scale.

During one of her visits to St. Clerans, John had Anjelica sit for a portrait, a brief exercise of one of his first talents to be developed. Anjelica, like most adolescents, didn't like the way she looked. She particularly hated her nose. English *Vogue* wanted to photograph her. When Anjelica arrived at the appointed place, one of England's most famous models of the time was there. The model's nose was, in Anjelica's words, "very small and perfect." The tall, leggy teenager felt totally intimidated in the presence of what she considered perfect beauty—finely chiseled features, blond hair, blue eyes.

While John made picture after picture, Ricki got on with her life. She had Allegra, the daughter who has the Huston name, although John Huston is certainly not her father. Later John Huston would write: "Also during our separation, Ricki had a daughter, Allegra, born in London in 1964. She bears my name and is as dear to me as Tony, Anjelica, and Danny."

Huston was in Rome when Allegra was born, finishing up work on *The Bible*. Zoe Sallis, Danny's mother, played a minor part in the film. Ricki's parents came over from New York to be with her when the baby was born, and Tony was also in London at the time. Anjelica was in Ireland, at boarding school.

The life Ricki fashioned for herself in London was one of serenity and beauty. "My mother's houses were always beautiful," Anjelica says, but behind the simplicity of that statement is the memory of the special ambience only a particularly gifted woman can create.

Ricki Soma Huston seems to have possessed

Humphrey Bogart and Walter Huston in John Huston's classic film *The Treasure of the Sierra Madre*, which won Walter an Oscar for Best Supporting Actor and his son John an Oscar for Best Director—the first family "double play" in Academy Award history. (Phototeque)

John Huston and Evelyn Keyes making beautiful music together. Keyes later wrote a bestselling "kiss and tell" autobiography, *Scarlet O'Hara's Younger Sister.*
(Pictorial Parade)

Jennifer Jones and Walter and John Huston on location for *We Were Strangers.* It was Jones's end-of-shooting gift to John, a chimpanzee named China, that helped break up his marriage to Evelyn Keyes. Keyes left and the chimp stayed.

Fatherhood comes to John Huston with the arrival of Walter Anthony Huston (Tony) in April of 1950. Wife number four, the beautiful ex-ballerina Ricki Soma Huston, looks on.

(Pictorial Parade)

A rough road for Anjelica in *A Walk With Love and Death*, the film her father directed her in when she was seventeen. Here she listens to her director father on location outside of Vienna.

(Pictorial Parade)

Like father, like son. Tony, age twelve, plays a key role in his father's suspense film *The List of Adrian Messenger*.

John Huston and Jack Nicholson in *Chinatown*, a film that brought the two big men in Anjelica's life together as co-actors.

A trio with something to smile about: Jack Nicholson and Anjelica, co-stars in *Prizzi's Honor*, with director John Huston at Beverly Hills's Motion Picture Academy for the premiere of the movie that would make Anjelica a star.

(Janet Gough/Celebrity Photo)

Anjelica Huston as Maerose Prizzi, wearing "the full stick" in a black dress trimmed with the Schiaparelli pink that Anjelica and her father simultaneously decided was perfect for her first big scene in *Prizzi's Honor*.

(Globe Pictures)

"We're proud of Pop," Anjelica and Jack Nicholson (with a classic Nicholson expression) seem to be saying at the 11th Annual American Film Institute Tribute honoring John Huston. Nicholson's affection for her father makes him "like family," Anjelica says.

Stand-in for father: Anjelica, with Richard Chamberlain and Faye Dunaway, accepts a Golden Globe Award for her father at the 43rd annual ceremony in January 1986. Huston won for *Prizzi's Honor*.

Sweet smile of success: Anjelica after winning an Oscar for Best Supporting Actress as Maerose in *Prizzi's Honor.*

(Smeal/Galella Ltd.)

Room at the top: Anjelica with Michael Douglas at a party in her honor after she won her Oscar.

(Anthony Savignano/Galella Ltd.)

A family portrait, Huston style. John Huston is shown at London's Heathrow Airport in 1985 with son Danny, daughter Anjelica, and his former wife, Cece Huston Jarre. Cece was the fifth Mrs. Huston, the wife in a marriage Huston said should never have happened. Huston is shown here in the wheelchair and portable oxygen tank that allowed him to continue to direct movies in spite of his worsening emphysema.

(Globe Photos)

A love letter to Ireland: *The Dead*, John Huston's last movie, based on the James Joyce short story, and starring his daughter in one of her most poignant roles.

(Phototeque)

the gift for making objects "hers"—making them, not an affirmation of her worth, as are the objects some people own, but an extension of her, a reminder of her, a concrete part of the personality friends called "extraordinary and charming."

The living room in the "Little Venice" house was a case in point. She painted a mural that she called "distressed Irish skies," using gray-blue colors rubbed until they resembled skies seen through Irish mist. She collected a circle of young friends and became a Quaker, establishing a social life that revolved around intimate dinner parties she gave in her pretty, tranquil house.

People who knew Ricki during those years saw a touch of sadness beneath her charm. Huston had made her very unhappy, and whether she attributed it to the difference in age—he was, after all, twenty-four years older than she—or whether she attributed it to the life he created in Ireland, the end result was that she wanted her closest friends and companions to be young—and she hated Ireland.

Huston, when he came to London, stayed at Claridge's, not at the house. Not long after Allegra's birth the rest of the family and friends knew what Huston already did—that Ricki had "someone," a lover whose identity no one ever knew.

The first Huston child to join the director-father in a film was not Anjelica, but Tony, who played a role in *The List of Adrian Messenger*. Shot in 1962, the movie included a fox hunt during which Tony's character would be killed. Tony took jumps with ease that a stuntman failed at: a feat that must have suited Papa Huston right down to the ground. The press also noted that Tony imitated his father's dress and style, wearing Irish country clothes when away from the camera.

Tony and Anjelica were both excellent riders. Watching his daughter and her friends with horses convinced Huston that little girls who like horses can tame even the most difficult animal. Except in the case of a real killer, he believed, you couldn't find a better trainer for a problem mount than a little girl. (One can hardly resist wondering if the same little girls who tamed wild horses might become women who could tame wild men. Ricki had never ridden before they moved to Ireland, and though she eventually learned, she came a cropper many times before she mastered the art.)

As a citizen of Ireland, John Huston was fired with the idea of starting a real cinema industry in that country. To this view, he shot parts of four pictures there: *Moby Dick, The List of Adrian Messenger, The Bible*, and *Casino Royale*. In 1968, Huston filmed *Sinful Davey* entirely in Ireland. He tested Anjelica for the leading role as the young highwayman's lover but decided against using her. That decision spared her being in one of her father's failures for another year, until he made *A Walk With Love and Death*, a film that was received with great praise and excitement in Paris, but which failed everywhere else.

Make no mistake, Huston said. In Hollywood language a film succeeds only if it makes money. Huston felt that there was "a certain purity" about *A Walk With Love and Death*, and *New Yorker* critic Pauline Kael liked it. But as a vehicle to launch his daughter as an actress—which is the reason Huston gave at the time for making the film in the first place—he couldn't have made a worse choice.

Anjelica knew at the time that if Huston had not been her father, she would never have been given the role. Since early childhood, when she and Ricki visited John on location in Tobago where he was shooting *Heaven Knows, Mr. Allison*, Anjelica had taken for granted the fact that what her father did for a living was make movies. Other children's fathers went to work in offices, or in the fields—hers made films. The actors and actresses that came in and out of her life were like anyone else's coworkers—some became friends, some didn't. But it was all just part of her routine existence.

At about the time Huston made *A Walk With Love and Death*, he told a reporter that while he didn't have a formal philosophy about how to live, he would say that "I never do anything that doesn't entertain me." His list of things he liked best began with "highly seasoned things, both foods and people." No wonder Huston's real interest in his children seems to have begun as they approached adulthood—and less wonder that when he and Anjelica finally clicked, she was a highly seasoned, dynamite lady in her thirties.

A Walk With Love and Death takes place in 1358 and tells the story of a young student and a girl on a trek through France. The Hundred Years' War had been going on almost twenty years, the terrain is devastated. Though set in the fourteenth century, the novel the film is based upon is meant by its author, Hans Koningsberger, to have a modern message against war.

For the role of the student-hero, Huston chose Assaf Dayan, the son of Moshe Dayan, at that time the Israeli defense minister. Assaf had had a tour of duty in the Israeli army, some bits and pieces of acting experience in Tel Aviv and Rome—but what he had going for him as far as Huston was concerned were "a kind of nobility and intelligence, a good face, and lovely manners." He also had a price on his head. As the son of Moshe Dayan, Assaf could be the target for Palestinians. Huston thus had to shoot the picture with no insurance on the leading man because 20th Century-Fox, the producing company, couldn't find any insurer who would cover him.

With typical grandeur John Huston told the press that he believed himself to be the only person in the history of films who had directed his father, his daughter, and himself. And when a dubious reporter asked Huston in September of 1968 if Anjelica could act, Huston said that of course she could, she did it all the time. Media attention naturally settled on the film, and Huston kept it supplied with typically Huston remarks. Of the casting of a real princess as a peasant in the film, Huston said, "I couldn't find anyone else who looked like a peasant."

Filming was plagued with riots and revolution. They began filming in France, only to run into student riots that totally disrupted Paris.

Finding it impossible to film in France, Huston moved to Vienna, Austria, with the idea of shooting the movie in a village just across the Czechoslovakian border. Then the Czechs began *their* revolt, the Russians moved in troops—and Huston and his entourage moved on to Italy, where the movie was finally made.

The coincidence of riots and protests occurring just when he was making a movie about protest colored Huston's filming, so that the modern message—one paralleling the events in the film to Vietnam and the civil rights movement in the U.S.—became clearer.

To an old hand like Huston, moving from one chaotic country to another was old hat. To daughter Anjelica, reared in quiet tranquillity, filming would have been enough of an experience without having to flee riots and revolutions. Summing up how she felt when shooting finally started, she said that sometimes she felt scared, and sometimes she didn't. But it was easier to scream or to cry than it was to be still and jolly.

She had watched others begin acting too early. Commenting that she had never wanted to make films when she was a child, she noted how hard it is to get away from a child-star image. And although the press respected Anjelica both for her horsemanship in handling the huge Noriker horses her father used in the film, and for her poise and intelligence when faced with reporters and photographers, Anjelica herself apparently went through the filming of *A Walk With Love and Death* in a state midway between panic and misery.

"It's really hard to make a movie on another person's territory," she would say later. "Especially when that person is your father. . . I couldn't speak up properly or understand properly, and maybe I didn't want to. It's hard being directed by one's father; he was impatient, and at the time I had no point of view, I never let on what I wanted for myself."

Jack Nicholson, talking about Anjelica's first movie experience many years later, voiced the opinion that John Huston cast Anjelica in the film—and announced her role to the press before he even told her—because he was "hoping to get his children to the point where they could see that all father-child roles were off, that he was just a man dealing with events." And in a comment that does much to explain why, when John Huston saw his daughter's relationship with Nicholson developing, he suggested to her that "we marry this man," Nicholson added that one of the difficulties an artist has is that while an artist doesn't want to exclude his family from his life, on the other hand "you don't want your family and your circumstances to intervene with your art."

Despite Anjelica's fears, Huston believed she had real talent. He said that film acting demands that an actor or actress be able to reveal "through the eyes . . . a glimpse of the real meaning of the character. It is not technique or professionalism, just truth. Garbo had it. Monroe had it. I can see it in Anjelica."

Huston spoke those words in 1968. It would be almost twenty years before his faith was vindicated in *Prizzi's Honor*.

Something Anjelica said in an interview featuring her and Joan Buck the year *Prizzi's Honor* and Joan's novel *Daughter of the Swan* came out gives a clue as to that inner spark John Huston saw. "I think I live a lot of lives at the same time," Anjelica said. "I've done that ever since I was a child." Saying that she sometimes felt as though characters from a B movie lived inside her, Anjelica commented that the "nature of acting is that one is many characters and jumps from one skin to another as a way of life." The line between acting and living blurs, it can be difficult to be aware of the thoughts of all these characters at any given time—and "sometimes one of my characters overrules one of my other characters." Anjelica at that time was, as she said, "trying to get them all to harmonize." But she was finding it "a hell of a job . . . like driving a coach."

Still, that ability to be someone else, to get in touch with these characters living inside her, carried her through the filming of *A Walk With Love and Death*, even if, as she remembers, "the first day I was out of my mind. My heart was going boom, boom, boom."

But it was still not a good experience. Even John Huston said later that "it might have been a mistake" to cast Anjelica in that part. Anjelica did not have to wait years to know her father had made a mistake. She knew it from the first, when she read the story and thought it "impossibly corny." The progression of events confirmed all her worst fears about the project, a project she couldn't say no to without offending her father.

In the early stages of filming, Anjelica thought

she looked good—but the more she hated the part, the more her emotions affected the way she looked. When she and costar Assaf Dayan watched the finished film, all alone in an empty screening room, they laughed to the point of hysteria. Under that laughter lay a lot of pain, at least on Anjelica's part. She and her father had not gotten along well during filming; she stayed away from him as much as she could, he didn't have a great deal to say to her. Ricki made one trip over, a trip that apparently didn't make matters any better. Anjelica hated Vienna, hated the role, didn't learn her lines, and thought she would never act again. If John Huston was trying, as Jack Nicholson surmised, to announce to Anjelica that the days of being father-daughter were over, and that from now on he "was just a man dealing with events," he succeeded with a vengeance. *A Walk With Love and Death* failed at the box office, failed to make Anjelica an actress—and drove a wedge into an already tenuous relationship.

Once filming was completed, in the winter of 1968, Anjelica returned to London. At seventeen, she recalls being in a stage where she avoided her parents, even her mother, to whom she was genuinely devoted. That stage is a natural condition of adolescence, as the child goes through girlhood and comes to the point of passage into adulthood. Even with a life so different from that of most adolescents, Anjelica probably would have completed her passage and at some point found the old closeness to her mother once again, had fate not intervened so traumatically only a few months later, when Ricki died. As Anjelica said, the fact that she and her mother had been going through an awkward time made Ricki's death, when it came, particularly terrible.

But no matter how awkward daughter Anjelica might have felt their relationship was, mother Ricki still reached out. A good friend of Ricki's, Tony Richardson, asked Anjelica to read for Ophelia in the production of *Hamlet* he was doing with Nicol Williamson. (Was this Ricki's way of counterbalancing John Huston's "gift" of the role in *A Walk With Love and Death*?) Although Anjelica lost out to Marianne Faithful, she was asked to understudy, and because Marianne was sick, she got to play the part a good number of times.

The character inside Anjelica who emerged to play Ophelia isn't hard to name: she is Grief. Grief onstage for Ophelia's father, whom her beloved Hamlet has killed, grief offstage for her mother, whose life ended on January 29, 1969. She had been on her way to Rome, where John was working on new projects. The driver of the car was a musician, Brian Anderson, a twenty-nine-year-old whose role in Ricki's life remained forever a mystery. All that was known was that he and Ricki were driving through France on *Route Nationale* 67 at dusk, two hundred miles south of Paris, when Anderson, apparently losing control of the sports car he drove, crashed head-on into a van.

Police and firemen worked an hour to get them out of the wreckage. Brian had severe facial lacerations; the driver of the van, Gilles Marcoux, lost his left leg; and Ricki Soma Huston, age thirty-nine, was dead.

There can be nothing as traumatic as sudden death—particularly when that person is your mother, on whom you have relied for love and approval and constancy since birth. And Ricki's death came at a particularly vulnerable time for Anjelica, right on the heels of her first test-by-fire under her father's direction, and when she was still struggling through the shoals of adolescence.

Anjelica did not even have the comfort of her other parent's presence when she learned that her mother was dead, nor did the message come from someone in the house with her, someone who might have held her and helped her over that first storm of grief. Already worried by the fact that they hadn't heard from Ricki—she had been calling every day to make sure young Allegra was all right—Anjelica answered the telephone the morning of January 30 to hear four words that changed the course of her life over the next few years.

"Your mother is dead," one of their tutors told her.

"I will never get over it as long as I live," Anjelica said sixteen years later, and even at that distance, grief and fury at the loss still raged. Trying to describe how she felt, Anjelica recalls that it was as though everything that belonged to Ricki—the house, the furniture, her clothes—had died, too. Their colors were faded, their textures dulled.

As though, Anjelica said, someone had deliberately tarnished everything in the house. The light had gone out of it, there was no brightness left.

Anjelica went to rehearsal for *Hamlet* that day in January: there seemed to be nothing else she could do. She told Tony Richardson what had happened, recalling that all she felt was a "mishmash of emotions." John was in Rome and had to take the train. He couldn't fly because even at that time his lungs were too bad. Anjelica remembers that when she and Tony met their father at Victoria Station, "I thought he was going to drop dead."

His health had always been a concern: people kept talking about Huston's health during the whole of Anjelica's childhood. "It always seemed to me that his health was quite fragile," she said. "He had emphysema; he'd go riding and have falls; he was drinking a bit—never a hair-of-the-dog man, but he could certainly put some away."

The question of Ricki's health never came up, Anjelica said. "So when she was killed, it was an unearthly, shattering blow—the kind of shock you simply don't get over. It's unparalleled in my life."

Huston, too, seemed as numb and bewildered as his children. He made the arrangements for Ricki's funeral, performed in the Quaker community she had joined. When it was over, he went back to work, Tony stayed on at London University awhile and then dropped out, and Anjelica went into a period of grief and depression that lasted, she said, almost seven years. Of the three, only Allegra's life stayed on keel. At four too young to really understand what had happened, and well cared for by her nurse, Maricela Hernandez, she went through that awful time in relative tranquillity.

John Huston said almost nothing in public about Ricki's death. He did tell AP reporter Hal Boyle a few months later that now he just made pictures, rode horses, collected paintings and regrets. "Most of my regrets, however, are of such a private nature that they would hardly bear either repetition or printing." And of daughter Anjelica he said, "Anjelica was frantic after Ricki died. I didn't know how to reach her, what to do. It was a very difficult time."

What he did do was to send Allegra and her nurse to Ireland, where they continued to live until a few years later when Huston finally sold St. Clerans, and to take Anjelica to New York for a promo tour of *A Walk With Love and Death*. Anjelica said this tour was something she did for her father in the old "the show must go on" tradition. It proved to be the final wrong thing in a whole sequence of wrong things. Critics called her "wooden and frozen," she remembers, and many years later she was still hard put to disentangle her grief for her mother from the way those reviews and that first film made her feel. The end result, she believes, is that through her reaction to two terrible experiences, one professional and one profoundly personal, she became the "bundle of fears" only *Prizzi's Honor* would release.

But at age seventeen, thrust suddenly into the adult world where pain and grief and anger and loss are part of the *donnée*, Anjelica believed she would never act again.

CHAPTER 7

*R*ICKI'S death brought the Hustons together only temporarily. Soon John got involved in another movie, *Myra Breckinridge*, this time as an actor. Tony was off traveling with Buckminster Fuller, the architect and creative genius. John Huston had introduced the two: the meeting resulted in a year's employment for Tony, a year in which he went with Fuller on a campus lecture tour, recording and transcribing the lectures. Commenting on that year, Tony said that his father had a way of putting experiences in his children's way, innovative things that would benefit them, and always acting as though he had done nothing of the kind. If Tony had not gotten what he needed from London University, his father probably reasoned, let's see what a year under the private tutelage of one of this century's greatest thinkers can do.

And Anjelica was off on her own tack. Turning her back on acting, she bumped right into a modeling career, one that she would look back on fondly, saying she seems to be one of the few models who enjoyed doing what she did.

Richard Avedon, the noted photographer of the notable, gave Anjelica her entrée. He asked Anjelica to go to Ireland with him. "I was always attracted by modeling—beautiful women, the whole idea of the fairy princess thing. It seemed a lovely thing to do." Avedon took what Huston describes as "lots of beautiful pictures." Now she had a portfolio, one most novices would kill for. And though she had had no real training—still, there she was, with "all these Avedon pictures."

"All these Avedon pictures" became thirty pages in an issue of *Vogue*—after that, everyone wanted Anjelica. Says one commentator: "Overnight she became the hottest thing on Kodachrome." She posed for all the big names, including Helmut Newton and Guy Bourdin.

But although she loved the attention, the beautiful clothes—it must have been like playing "dress-up" again with her mother's Balenciagas—she hated the way she looked. "Day after day I shared a mirror with the world's most beautiful women and stared at eyes that were bigger than mine, noses that were smaller. I cried and cried because I thought I was ugly, but now when I see those photographs, I think I look absolutely wonderful!"

Then a man came into her life, photographer Bob Richardson. He took lots of pictures, too—and he also took Anjelica into his personal life. The relationship that began when Anjelica was seventeen and Richardson was in his early forties would last four years. Modeling took Anjelica into a new world, one much more her own. Soon after her New York debut she talked about the differences between London and New York. London "is a village in comparison to New York," she said, adding that although she loved London, New York is "the only exciting city there is." It was honest, she thought. And "mythically ugly." But exciting. And so was modeling, which she found inspiringly competitive.

How nice it must have been for John Huston's daughter to feel that she had found a patch of sunshine not of her father's making. If she had felt pared down, bared and defenseless, as she said later, by her experience acting in *A Walk With Love and Death*, she would feel sheltered and shielded by the experience of print modeling. The film camera wants that moment of truth John Huston spoke of, that glimmer of the real character lying just behind the actor's eyes. The camera shooting high-fashion print work wants nothing of the kind. A beautiful rack on which garments can be hung. A persona that creates an ambience. All of this is on the surface, and behind the carefully made-up face all emotions, including pain and grief, can hide.

Tony and Anjelica both saw Stanley Kubrick's *2001* and thought their father should see it. Huston did, then made a movie of what he considered the same genre: one in which technology is more important than character. This film, released in 1970, was *The Kremlin Letter*. Following that was *Fat City*, a film premiered in New York City in August 1972, just before Huston's sixty-sixth birthday.

Lillian Ross, a *New Yorker* magazine columnist, wrote about the occasion. She said that both Tony and Anjelica, on hand for the screening and party at the Museum of Modern Art, "have faces that remind us of their mother, the late Enrica Soma Huston, who was a strikingly beautiful woman." Anjelica, Ross said, was working as a model in New York and wore a "white chiffon shimmery gown and pearls." Commenting that Anjelica came up and hugged her father from behind, Ross said Huston "looked happy." Three and a half years after Ricki's death, and maybe the worst of the trauma was behind them. Certainly Tony, at six foot four, seemed to be in a good place.

Both Huston men, Ross reported, wore "crisp seersucker jackets, the father with a white shirt and a rakish black bow tie, the son with a brick-red shirt and a multicolored Art Nouveau tie." And they looked at each other with "unconcealed admiration, very much the way the late Walter Huston and John used to look at each other," Ross wrote. Tony was still training falcons, an art he had begun at age ten. And he was still writing poetry and had begun to write prose. And, his father said, Tony had also been going to all the museums. Reading the piece gives one the feeling that Huston was reminded of his own first summer in New York, when, four years younger than his son was at that time, he had felt the special magic that city has. Certainly it is clear that Tony and John Huston had a good rapport; the Ross piece ends with these lines: "Huston ducked out of the party . . . Tony . . . walked out . . . with him . . . Tony's face was glowing with enthusiasm . . . the two men hugged each other. 'It was the best, Dad,' Tony said. Huston . . . looked at him, then drew him close again and gave his deep laugh over the younger man's shoulder. Tony then drew away and looked straight into his father's eyes. 'It was really the best, Dad,' he said. 'And you know I don't lie.'"

Anjelica hugs her father from behind—Tony gets a close-up. Father and daughter were still not on the same path, and it would be another twelve years before they were.

Someone else was at the opening of *Fat City*—Celeste Shane, known as Cece, the woman who would become John Huston's fifth wife. She came from California with Darlene Pearson, wife of John's old friend Bill, the jockey, and with Bill Gardner. Tall, slim, big-eyed, and divorced, Cece was from the nonmovie, horse-loving circle of friends so important to John all of his life. The daughter of a car rental executive, Cece wanted to act—and to be a leader in the Hollywood social set. Now Huston's production secretary, Cece married John a week after *Fat City* opened. A Santa Monica judge married the thirty-one-year-old bride and sixty-six-year-old groom.

If anyone thought John Huston was making a mistake, it wasn't recorded. Later he would say that marrying the fifth time was like putting his finger in a sea snake's mouth. "I survived," he said. "But barely."

Anjelica liked Cece. Or so she said to the New York gossip columnists who pressed her for an opinion. "I'm truly thrilled," she said. "She's a really lovely lady and I hope she changes his life."

The new Mrs. Huston, less than half her husband's age, had a son, Collin, only a year younger than Allegra Huston. Collin had cerebral palsy and required the care of medical specialists. That factor, combined with Cece's antipathy to everything about Ireland, led to the first major change Cece would make in Huston's life. St. Clerans was put up for sale. After all, John reasoned, St. Clerans had been meant as a home for Tony and Anjelica. They didn't need it anymore—and neither did he. His new family, composed of Cece and Collin and Anjelica, would live in Puerto Vallarta. Huston would still be an expatriate and safe from Uncle Sam's income tax laws, and Cece could take Collin into the States for treatment.

John Huston respected his new wife's devotion to her son, but that emotion did present him with a situation entirely new in the Huston experience. Whereas in his marriage to Ricki, he put her and the children in a safe place where he could find them when he wanted them, Cece put Collin's health first. She and Collin accompanied Huston to Europe to film *The Mackintosh Man*, but returned to Los Angeles when Collin's condition worsened and English physicians advised Cece to take him home. And though the marriage would go on for three years, it should have been apparent then and there that Huston had taken on a woman who did not put him first. Since marriage to him was, admittedly, never easy, given his womanizing, his concentration on his work, his adherence to a lifestyle that suited him with little compromise to accommodate anyone else, it is no wonder that the Cece Shane–John Huston union ended three years after it was formed.

But while it lasted, Cece turned some of her attention to another Huston child, Anjelica, who had broken up with Bob Richardson shortly after her father's fifth marriage. The end of that relationship occurred in a John Huston–directed scenario. As Anjelica says, she and Bob broke up at the airport in Mexico City, after going along with "this crazy idea that my father had that we all go deep-sea fishing together in Puerto Vallarta for a few days."

Anjelica told Bob Richardson good-bye—and added the whole modeling scene for good measure. Bob was too much a part of that life. She stayed in California, not really doing anything, and then Cece began introducing her to eligible young men, arranging blind dates that Anjelica found "all very embarrassing."

Now twenty-one, Anjelica was hardly the

grief-stricken adolescent critics had found wooden and unresponsive as she stumbled her way through a promotion tour for a film she hated in the months after her beloved mother's death.

She had tested herself in a very tough arena—Anjelica told the truth when she said she shared a mirror every day with some of the most beautiful women in the world—and she had come out of it a winner. She had attracted and held the interest of a man more than twice her age—a feat her mother, too, had pulled off. And though at that point in her life she was, as she said, very tired, and in need of a rest, the image she projected, in the words of the next man to enter her life, was "pure class."

That man was Jack Nicholson.

They met in 1973 at a party at Nicholson's house in the mountains above Beverly Hills. Although Nicholson could see the scars beneath the beautiful facade, he also soon discovered the many and varied components of Anjelica's personality. "She's got this great natural sophistication," he would say. "But she could live in Alaska with a guy who hunts wolves and do just fine." Shades of her father, who, according to Lauren Bacall, didn't care if he ever left Africa after filming *The African Queen*, and yet who was equally at home dressed to the nines at a Galway Hunt Ball.

As for Anjelica—she saw Jack's eyes. "They were kind, and his whole face lit up when he smiled," she remembers of that first meeting.

It didn't take long for the two to be head over heels in love. A friend reports that Anjelica seemed "engulfed" by Nicholson: a man the friend described as "an older man who was just as charismatic as her father—and just as big a chaser."

Anjelica proved less vulnerable to the constant reports of Jack's women than her mother had been: perhaps she had absorbed by some kind of psychic osmosis her father's attitudes. There are not that many people who understand the full dimension of the human personality, nor can tolerate the fact that some people may require many experiences and relationships to search out and develop every aspect of their inner selves. Some of these experiences and relationships may be superficial and quite brief, others may work at a deeper level and continue for some time. And it is possible, as Nicholson and Anjelica Huston have shown, for all these other experiences and relationships to serve as mere threads against the broader fabric of the relationship that means the most.

Anjelica was extremely tired when she met Jack Nicholson: she wanted to rest. Nicholson was struck not only by Anjelica, but by John Huston. As Nicholson himself was fatherless, this great director–father figure seemed the perfect person to complete a trio of interwoven needs and dependencies. "What a duo Nicholson and Huston make, in a father-son affinity that must be as complicated as it is comforting for Anjelica," an observer commented.

At any rate, in 1973, moving in with Jack Nicholson and letting the dynamics of his world provide enough energy for both of them seemed the right thing to do. She would take a year off, she thought—a year that turned into quite a few more.

In the beginning, Nicholson said, he called Anjelica "Anjelica the Moan" because she deprecated herself so constantly and drained her own psychic energy by being so incredibly hard on herself. And Jack's lifestyle turned out to be less restful than Anjelica might have hoped.

At first the relationship had a balance that it later lacked. Jack went to Europe to make a film, *The Passenger*, and Anjelica took a modeling job there, which put them in the same geographical context, so they could see each other, and yet it was also a situation in which Anjelica as well as Jack had work to do.

Things changed when they returned to California. There were, as Nicholson said, "a lot of clarifications and adjustments we had to make." Anjelica found it hard to take all the attention that came Nicholson's way—when the phone rang, it was always about him, or for him. She thought her life with her father had prepared her for living with an actor whose schedule was consistent only in its erraticism. What she failed to realize was that although her father had flitted in and out of her life, her mother had always been there. Now she had to put up with a living arrangement that would, in Nicholson's words, allow them to be in tandem and yet still have their freedom.

A major problem probably lay in the fact that Anjelica needed Jack more at that point than he needed her: he had a booming career, she had nothing.

She reacted to the uncertainties in their relationship by seeing other people occasionally, and at one point leaving Jack completely for Ryan O'Neal. She came back, "more mature and more beautiful," Jack said. He could see new dimensions in Anjelica every time they renewed their relationship: he remained the "wild man" with a reputation for staying out late and going off after another woman whenever he felt closed in.

The same year that Anjelica met Nicholson, Jack worked in Roman Polanski's film *Chinatown*, in which John Huston also had a third-billing role. Polanski and Nicholson got along in the casual, spontaneous way people of similar instincts working on the same project get along: at one point, while Polanski was looking for a place to live, he stayed with Nicholson. It was this connection between Polanski and Nicholson that would, in March of 1977, get Anjelica involved in an ugly brush with the law.

The main actor in the incident was Roman Polanski, who was charged by a grand jury with furnishing a controlled substance to a minor; committing a lewd or lascivious act; having unlawful sexual intercourse; perversion; sodomy; and rape by use of drugs. The girl in question was a thirteen-year-old whom Polanski was photographing with the idea of her possible inclusion in a series he was shooting for *Vogue* magazine.

The incident leading to Polanski's arrest occurred the second day of shooting. According to Polanski, he took his subject to Jack Nicholson's house on the southwest side of Mulholland Drive because the natural light in the hills was good there. Roman called Nicholson, whose answering service put him through to a neighbor of Jack's. There were three houses in the compound: the woman's, Marlon Brando's, and Nicholson's. The woman knew Polanski, who had stayed with Nicholson on occasion, and agreed to push the buzzer that would open the electronically controlled gate so he could get in.

The neighbor met Polanski and let him into the house. Anjelica wasn't there, but the woman said she would be back soon. (Actually, Anjelica and Nicholson had just broken up again, and she was not actually living in the house at the time.)

What happened after Polanski and the girl went into the house has never been clarified. Polanski voluntarily took deportation to avoid going to trial, so the discrepancies between his story as told in his autobiography and the charges the grand jury made could not be resolved.

At any rate, Anjelica's involvement in the incident began when Roman noticed the light on the telephone in the TV room go on and realized that someone else—probably Anjelica—was in the house. He went to the door and called to her, and she answered him from another room. Some of the accessories used in the shoot were in the living room with Anjelica. When they went to retrieve them, Roman introduced the girl to Anjelica, explaining that they were in a hurry to leave because the girl had had an asthma attack. Anjelica got back on the phone, and Roman left.

By late the next afternoon, Roman Polanski was under arrest. He had one Quaalude on him;

the police found others in his hotel suite, which they searched with the authority of a warrant. They had another search warrant, too—this one for Jack Nicholson's house. The police drove with Polanski to Nicholson's house and rang the bell, but received no answer. Roman got out of the police car and climbed over the fence, opening the gate from the inside—something he had learned to do when he had stayed at Nicholson's and wanted to get inside late at night without waking anyone up. Thinking no one was home, he was surprised to see Anjelica lean out of a first-floor window as the cars came up to the house.

Roman explained the situation, and Anjelica came down to let them in. A search commenced. Roman showed the policemen around the lower floor of the house, and another one took Anjelica upstairs. "She came down a few minutes later, white-faced," Roman reported in his autobiography, *Roman*. "'They've got it,' she said." Anjelica referred to a small amount of cocaine in her purse. When they left the house for the West Los Angeles precinct on Purdue Avenue, Roman was in one car—and Anjelica was in another.

Roman had no contact with Anjelica in the days between his arrest and the grand jury appearance. Once the charges had been made, and he had been formally indicted, Roman and his lawyers went to work to prepare his defense. A crucial point in the prosecution's case would be Anjelica's testimony, Polanski's lawyer told him. Only she could put Polanski in the house and in the room. In his account of the events, Roman says that "after several days of suspense we learned that Anjelica had been granted immunity on all charges of drug possession in return for undertaking to give evidence for the prosecution." Although he says he couldn't really blame her "for accepting the deal," it left him "feeling slightly bitter."

Anjelica had a different view. Saying that it's illegal to testify "for" or "against" anyone, she states that she only told the truth. After all, Roman Polanski *was* in Nicholson's house, he *was* in the TV room—had Anjelica said he was not, she would have been guilty of perjury. Calling his error of judgment something she still resents, Anjelica adds, with typical Huston fairness, that when he signed her copy of his autobiography, *Roman*, to her with the words "No hard feelings," she thought that "was rather sweet."

Such incidents demonstrate clearly the difficulty most people who live in Hollywood, work there, and associate with other people who live and work there to the exclusion of people in other walks of life have with keeping both feet in the "real" world. More can happen in one week in a film actor's or actress's life than happens to "ordinary people" in a year—perhaps even a lifetime. On such an emotional roller coaster, it must be hard indeed to keep a focused vision, a direct path.

Here Anjelica Huston had just broken up with Nicholson, and immediately found herself involved with a Hollywood-type scandal just because she was literally in the wrong place at the wrong time. People who grow up aspiring to be film stars are possibly better able to accept the bizarre conditions that go with it. Anjelica at this point in time had no such aspirations. She had fallen in love with Nicholson and had submerged her life in his. Increasingly it wasn't working. She still felt "somewhat demoralized and paralyzed," unable to take charge of her own life.

And increasingly Anjelica realized that for all Jack Nicholson's strength and charisma, he had holes in his own past. In the early years of their relationship, Jack, who had grown up without knowing his father, found out that the "mother" and the "sister" who had reared him were in actuality his grandmother and mother. Such a discovery might have sent someone else into long-term psychotherapy. But like Anjelica, Nicholson believes that there are times when you have to "know when not to ask too many questions."

Perhaps as a result of having his childhood world turned upside down, or perhaps as a way of bonding himself to Anjelica's past, Nicholson took Anjelica to Ireland soon after he learned the truth about his own family. Anjelica had not seen St. Clerans since right after her mother's death. The place had of course been sold years before, and the new owners, opening their door to find Jack Nicholson wanting to go through the house, with Anjelica Huston besides, said no. Nicholson and Anjelica did walk over the grounds and came upon a gardener who had worked at St. Clerans in John Huston's time.

"He had Irish tears brimming in his eyes," Nicholson recalled. And since Anjelica by that time was a "weepy woman," Jack reported that he had a good time.

The "roots" trip was no more successful than anything else in settling Anjelica's self-doubts and getting her life into motion. For almost seven years she accepted being John Huston's daughter, and Jack Nicholson's girlfriend. Things didn't have to be that way. "It wasn't that I didn't know a great many directors," Anjelica said. At one point, when Jack was working with Warren Beatty on a movie called *The Fortune*, the director, Mike Nichols, asked Anjelica to test for a part. She refused. "Absolutely not," she told Nichols. "I don't want gifts from friends. I don't want handouts." And so she did not do the test.

It must have amazed women who would have sold every grandmother in sight to have Anjelica's connections in the industry to watch her not use them to the hilt. In fact, Anjelica herself said later that people thought she didn't want to work. Hollywood logic came up with that as the only possible reason she didn't appear in films: she must be satisfied with the status quo, because if she'd wanted to change it, one phone call would have done the job.

Then a casual comment by an old friend and yet another traumatic experience jolted Anjelica out of the doldrums and propelled her back into the mainstream of life.

She happened to be talking to Tony Richardson, with whom she had worked on *Hamlet* so many years before, at a party one night. He told her that in his opinion, she would never do anything about her acting. When she said nothing, only thinking to herself that she would do something at some point, he added, "It doesn't matter *what* you do. Actors *work*. You just *work*."

That alone got Anjelica moving a little—she took a few classes, began to send feelers out. She took whatever she could get, trying to overcome the handicap of always being identified through her father or Nicholson, trying to come out of the cloud of notoriety because of the Polanski business, trying to get known as an actress serious about her work.

She had small roles in movies like *Swashbuckler*—of which one critic said that the director had taken Anjelica Huston, a merely homely woman, and made her into a perfect horror—and *The Last Tycoon*. She took parts in TV series, appearing in "Laverne and Shirley" episodes and in a few segments of "Faerie Tale Theatre." She even worked as an extra in *Frances*, driving herself two and a half hours each way to location every day for three weeks. She found, as she said, that "work breeds work . . . although at a certain point you have to do a lot of stuff you don't love."

And then came the real turning point. Anjelica was in a wreck in 1980, a serious one. She had just put a tape in her car's tape deck; she wasn't wearing her seat belt, but as she shoved the tape into place, she remembered giving her mother tapes to take on that trip through France—and had a sudden feeling that maybe she should fasten her seat belt. She didn't. When a drunk driver on the wrong side of the road came bearing down on Anjelica, all she could see was two headlights. She went through the windshield, broke her nose badly, and required plastic surgery for six hours and a long convalescence. She convalesced at Nicholson's house—this was during the filming of *The Postman Always Rings Twice*, a movie in which she had a small role. (The reviews of the movie were almost uniformly bad. Few even mentioned Anjelica. *Newsweek* said: "Anjelica Huston pops up absurdly in the guise of a German lion tamer.") Jack was away filming, leaving Anjelica time and space to think about her life.

The thinking didn't come easily. One night she woke with convulsions, and despite desperate efforts to reach friends, she couldn't get anyone to answer "because they had all turned off their phones because they were tired of dealing with me."

That must have been a long, pain-filled, frightening night. But it might have been the night Anjelica Huston discovered, finally, that all the hard things and all the easy things and all the good things and all the bad things—we do alone. No one can live our lives for us, no one can take responsibility for what we must take care of ourselves.

Anjelica came out of that dark night knowing what it was she wanted to do with her life. "I wanted to act," she said. And this time—she meant it.

CHAPTER 8

ANJELICA'S resolve to take charge of her life began operating with her decision to study acting seriously. Others had suggested that she study: Lee Grant, directing Anjelica in a production of a Strindberg play some years before, had made the suggestion, and so had Jack Nicholson. After all her experience—she had, after all, played Ophelia in London and also in New York when the Richardson production moved there—it was a little like going back to kindergarten. But this time Anjelica had a teacher who would make all the difference.

There is a learning theory that says no one

really learns anything—masters it in a way that works—unless the lesson is offered at just the magic moment when mind, heart, and spirit are open and ready to learn. Peggy Feury entered Anjelica's life at just that magic moment. As a teacher she reinforced Anjelica's belief in herself and helped her establish self-confidence. She also taught Anjelica to be less demanding of herself, to be calmer about her work and about her own abilities. "I was very insecure and apt to overstate in my performance," Anjelica said. Above all, Peggy was kind. For perhaps the first time in her life Anjelica worked with someone on an even basis, with no emotional baggage to overload the exchange.

Another discovery helped Anjelica stop being so critical of her looks. She realized that her nose, which had been a kind of bête noire for so long, had, in taking the worst impact of the crash, probably saved the rest of her face. "I had newfound respect for my nose," she said.

And she learned her strengths as an actress— she has an instinct for a good story—as well as her weaknesses. It's hard for her to learn lines, for example. Not the actual process itself, but the getting started part of it. She compares it to manual labor, saying she always thinks it's going to be harder than it really is. Anjelica learned, too, the aspects of film work that are just plain tedious, such as the very long hours and the amount of time a performer waits until the scene he or she is in is filmed. "It's hard work keeping the energy up" during such long waits, Anjelica found.

But as her confidence in herself and in her

craft grew, she began to reach out. While Anjelica's role in *This Is Spinal Tap*, a satire of a British rock group's U.S. tour, was so small most reviewers didn't even mention her, the film itself got good reviews. Not an instant box office hit, it sort of grew on audiences, gradually building up a following. The important thing wasn't the size of Anjelica's role: the important thing was that the production itself was creative, solid work. She was working with good people, people who could affirm her new sense of self.

The new sense of self manifested itself in an important rite of passage when Anjelica moved out of Jack Nicholson's house and into one of her own. That move was not intended to weaken their relationship, which has gone on now for fifteen years, much longer than any of John Huston's marriages. Anjelica needed her own space, a space in which, when the phone rang, it was for her, about her. "Jack's life is very large," she commented. "It had a way of getting in the way of mine."

In 1983, Anjelica appeared in *The Ice Pirates*, a movie called a "dim-witted, slow-moving space spoof" by one critic. John Foreman directed the film, which even MGM, the distributor, didn't believe in—it held the movie for almost nine months after it was completed, waiting for a propitious time to release it. Anjelica's role, as, to quote Foreman, "the most terrifying swordswoman in the universe," didn't stand out for viewers—but it did for him. What he saw there made him believe that Anjelica would make the perfect Maerose Prizzi.

And by that time Anjelica agreed with him. "Some things are in your blood, I guess," she says about her reemergence as an actress. She found comedy a good place to be, in terms of work. "There's a wonderful karma in doing funny stuff," she says. "It doesn't mean you have to get goofy, but there is a subtle inner knowledge about doing comedy that makes you happy. It takes the weight off the work."

Maerose Prizzi proved to be the best of both worlds. Maerose had plenty of comic moments, but the role also gave Anjelica the opportunity to portray a whole range of feelings. The audience sees her seduced, abandoned, shrewish, spinsterish—and finally, lethally efficient. "This woman does not spend a lot of time questioning herself," Anjelica observed, "because her motives are so pure. She has a plan and she carries it out."

Director-father John Huston saw Maerose the same way. "She is like her grandfather, the Don. She is a Titan. She is going to take over the family and become the power behind the throne, the eternal matriarch."

Prizzi's Honor was a rite of passage for Anjelica Huston in more ways than one. First, of course, it proved once and for all that when she resolved to be an actress, she made exactly the right choice. And through the medium of acting, Anjelica and John Huston finally closed the last space between them.

Finding her father much more accessible and open than she ever had before—perhaps because she herself was both of these things—Anjelica grew steadily closer to the man who had missed her physical birth into the world the summer of 1951, but who acted as chief midwife when she was born as an actress through Maerose. "He's truly a man of honor, extremely loyal, extremely steadfast," she would say. "If one was ever in trouble, he would be there with no questions, and he has been for me; and in situations where one fears he might disapprove, he is surprisingly on one's side."

Shades of Walter Huston, in whose eyes son John could do no wrong!

Anjelica had waited a long, long time for that kind of approval from her father. She remembers that toward the end of filming *Prizzi*, John Huston called her one day to say she had done well in a scene they had filmed. "Afterwards," she said, "I realized I'd been waiting to hear that. It's something that will last me for ten years, and I'm sure other people working for him feel the same way."

That approval might have overcome Anjelica's own private "worst image of herself." She imagines herself sitting in a darkened movie theater watching herself in close-up, criticizing herself mercilessly, never satisfied with what she has done. After *Prizzi's Honor* the image could surely change. She might still find fault with what she saw on the screen—but there is a difference between an insecure novice's thinking she can do nothing right and a cool, talented, and skilled professional's thinking—"Well, it could have been done that way—or this way—or even that way."

Just before *Prizzi's Honor* came up, something

else happened that reinforced Anjelica's newfound confidence and self-esteem. A friend offered her the title role in *Tamara*, an experimental play by Canadian writer John Krizanc. The play's action centers around the arrival of the artist Tamara de Lempicka at the home of Gabriele D'Annunzio, the Italian playwright, novelist, and poet who died in 1938. The action truly follows all that happens— the drama takes place in ten separate rooms, and the audience follows actors from room to room, thus knowing only one of the many intricate subplots in the play. (Real aficionados returned over and over again until they had the entire story.) Anjelica went to a reading and immediately fell in love with the part, which called for beautiful clothes, "lots of French," and had all the rich potential that made her call it a "part made in heaven" for her.

Reading the part was one thing, getting it was another. When the call came, Anjelica remembers feeling "really great." The role would be a challenge. Each of the ten cast members has an individual story, a subplot that is followed to its end during the play. The audience chooses which character to follow: some nights a character might have three people following his/her story, another night half the audience might go along in his/her train.

Scenes and story lines overlap. Actors and audience pass other actors and their audience as they go from room to room, and occasionally several characters with their followers come together to witness the same scene. Moses Znaimer, the Canadian television and pop culture entrepreneur who produced *Tamara*, said, "Confident people believe in the validity of their choice and enjoy the story that they choose. People lacking in confidence are always sure that they're missing something."

So successful was the Los Angeles production of *Tamara* that it settled down for a run that went well into the fourth year. Anjelica did not stay with the play for that length of time, but she stayed long enough to attract good notices—and to win the 1985 Distinguished Performance Award from *Dramalogue Magazine* for her work in the play. Then, fast on that success, came Maerose Prizzi—and Anjelica's world was forever changed.

By this time Anjelica's relationship with Jack Nicholson had settled into a pattern that had, as one observer remarked, as much stability as most marriages, with a lot more sensitivity. Comments producer Bob Evans, "He [Jack] used to be a very big player—not even Warren Beatty has been so successful with women—but now that seems to have subsided." Evans went on to say that he thought Jack would never leave Anjelica—she is all he wants. Calling Nicholson a "glittering vagrant," Evans says that Huston's upbringing and culture gave Nicholson's life the foundation it needed. She's refined him, Evans says, summing up the relationship in these words: "The man is a diamond, and she's given him a beautiful setting."

And John Foreman, who produced *Prizzi's Honor*, sees a great respect in Nicholson's attitude toward Anjelica. He values her, Foreman says, doing everything but rising when she comes into the room. She's at the center of his life—he'd give her anything she asked for. A home—marriage—all of it. (Actually, Anjelica has refused expensive jewelry many times over. She surrounds herself with beautiful things—but she likes to get them herself.) Foreman thinks Nicholson and Huston are much nicer to each other than most people who are legally married. Apparently what the two have between them doesn't need anything to affirm it, or to make it work.

Nicholson agrees. Commenting that Anjelica is, after all, only two minutes away, he says that they do talk about marriage, but that it's just never become critical. They have a vital relationship, one that keeps growing. And with two very busy professionals, having time and space to themselves is important. Nicholson doesn't see Anjelica as much as in the days before she catapulted to stardom: she's more involved in her own projects, just as he is in his. But that balances the relationship, making a positive change from the early days when Anjelica needed Jack to fill all the empty spaces, and he had many other resources to help fill his.

Even on location in Brooklyn for *Prizzi's Honor*, they stayed in separate hotels. They both had their work cut out for them—neither had fully understood the comic values of the film when they began work—and Anjelica found that Jack "had a little too much of the hit man in him" sometimes. It was better to be away from him then.

Oddly enough, for a relationship that had

been going on a dozen years when Anjelica won her Oscar, the moviegoing public knew little enough about it. Or perhaps not so odd, since until that time the moviegoing public had not paid that much attention to Anjelica Huston, although it had paid a great deal of attention to Jack Nicholson.

After Academy Award night everyone wanted to know more about Anjelica—and more about this perfect example of how opposites attract. And attract and attract and attract.

Nicholson's background, after all, could not be more different from Anjelica's. While she grew up in the fairy-tale castle in Galway, Jack grew up in Neptune, New Jersey. He was born on April 22, 1937, and he would be almost forty years old before he found out that the woman he called mother, a beautician whose shop was in her house, and the alcoholic sign painter he called father, a man who lived separately from Jack and his mother, were in fact his grandparents. His mother, June, later a dancer in *Earl Carroll Vanities*, had only been seventeen when he was born. And although June Nicholson must have known who Jack's father was, no one else ever did.

A bright, talented boy growing up in such circumstances may have a lot of choices—but most boys choose the same thing. Rebel against everything and everybody and make them as miserable as possible in the process. Jack took that same modus operandi west to Hollywood, arriving in the mid-Fifties, and setting out to make a name for himself. He did that, although in the beginning the name was associated with controlled substances and a crowd of rebellious friends. Then he made *Easy Rider*, the Nicholson equivalent of Huston's *Prizzi's Honor*.

Tales of the swath Nicholson cut through Hollywood in the years following *Easy Rider* are reminiscent of John Huston himself. Perhaps that's one reason the two had such an affinity, an affinity that made Nicholson remark once, "When John Huston dies, I'll cry for the rest of my life."

Nicholson could raise hell all night and work like a pro all day; his activities at night gave him a national reputation for womanizing and drug use, and his work by day gave him increasing stature as an actor. Films like *Five Easy Pieces* and *One Flew Over the Cuckoo's Nest* established Nicholson solidly in the ranks of Hollywood's most gifted actors, a ranking Anjelica Huston confirms.

"Jack is a very rare and special being," she says. "Most actors are vain and egotistical, but Jack is very sensible . . . he's at home with himself, and when you're with him, you feel as if you've come home. You feel he's *family*."

Anjelica believes that Jack's audiences sense this, that his star power lies in the fact that audiences believe he understands what *they* are feeling. Audiences sense a loyalty, and they give it back to him.

The stars must have been in the right configuration that night in 1973 when Anjelica Huston and Jack Nicholson met, particularly when Anjelica's state of mind at the time is considered. But twelve years later, in the glow of *Prizzi's Honor*, the woman who found in Jack Nicholson's self-assurance a "homeplace" for herself had one of her own. She had worked with two powerful males, her father and her lover, who had been so significant a part in shaping her life. She had worked through her professional fears, and she had worked through her private relationships. She emerged a star—a woman full grown—and perhaps best of all, a working actress, with a schedule all her own.

The next project was *Captain Eo*, a cartoonish spectacle directed by Francis Coppola. Anjelica plays a witch, with Michael Jackson in the other major role. George Lucas produced the technically advanced 3-D laser film for exclusive showing at Disney World. Anjelica had a blast flying around and carrying on in a film where she began as a witch and ended up as a queen.

Fast on the heels of *Captain Eo* came *Gardens of Stone*, also directed by Francis Coppola. Her first real lead role, the part of Samantha Davis, is a complete contrast to brassy, self-assured Maerose Prizzi. And *Gardens of Stone* could hardly be more different from *Prizzi's Honor*.

Based on the novel by Nicholas Proffitt, *Gardens of Stone* is the story of three men assigned to the Army's Old Guard at Arlington National Cemetery. The Old Guard is the highly trained, highly specialized ceremonial unit that helps bury this nation's honored dead. Set in 1968–69, *Gardens* shows the Vietnam war from a stateside viewpoint, telling a tale of military disillusionment with a war politicians constrained the armed forces from winning.

James Caan is Clell Hazard, the sergeant Samantha Davis, a *Washington Post* reporter and peace activist, loves. James Earl Jones is Hazard's sidekick, Sergeant Major Goody Nelson. The young man Hazard loves like a son is played by D. B. Sweeney, with Mary Stuart Masterson as the colonel's daughter who loves him.

The thrust of the movie's story is Jackie Willow's (Sweeney) desire to go to Vietnam where the fighting is. Hazard and Nelson know that this war is different—but despite all they say, Willow is unswerving. Since the film opens with Willow's military funeral at Arlington, the audience knows from the beginning how the story will turn out. Though some critics saw this as a weakness, others believed that the story was not as important to Coppola as the message of the movie. "This film deals with family relationships," Caan says. "That family happens to be the United States Army. It's a timeless story of a teacher and his pupil, of a father and his son, of a man and the woman he loves."

For Anjelica Huston, the film was much more than that. As one reviewer said, Vietnam is the war we can't forget, but the war Anjelica Huston could hardly remember. She had, after all, been three thousand miles away from the United States in 1968–69. Making *Gardens of Stone* gave her a new awareness of Vietnam, and not only because of the content of the film.

Her driver had fought in the war, and her

wardrobe lady's fiancé had gone to Vietnam and never come back. Although the military aspects of *Gardens* were unfamiliar to Anjelica, the theme of the love story, that two very different people could fall in love, appealed to her very much. "I liked Samantha," Anjelica said. "She was a good girl, sweet and strong and full of heart. And I wanted to be able to say the things that she said, that war is genocide."

Working with Coppola proved to be quite different from working with her father. For one thing, unlike most movie directors, Coppola gives his cast at least two weeks of rehearsals before he starts filming. They rehearse the movie in the chronological sequence in which the story occurs rather than in the out-of-order sequence films are normally shot in. And both during rehearsal and during shooting, actors may improvise dialogue if they feel it is necessary to flesh out the script.

The result was a Samantha that most critics praised highly. Anjelica turned in a performance called "full, boldly acted," which was, in the view of some, surprising, since despite her Oscar she had never had a leading role. Another critic praised her performance by saying that she was so good you wished she had a larger role. And most critics found the love affair between Hazard-Caan and Davis-Huston "one of the great adult love stories of our time."

Others found the movie static—or in the obvious phrase, "stonelike." "While Hazard and Sam console each other over the death of a friend," one critic wrote, "they race through their tears, decide

Hazard should ship out to Vietnam again, and agree to get married, all in the space of a few minutes."

Anjelica commented on the difficulty of fitting the many interwoven stories within the film into under two hours. "It was an extremely big undertaking," she said. She saw the film, as did Coppola, as dealing with family. And that is a theme close to her heart. "Family is the most important thing. Either the one you come from, or the one you create for yourself—whether it's a movie company or bloodlines." Perhaps it is this innate sense of family that made Anjelica so sympathetic to Samantha, who is the surrogate mother to Jackie Willow, just as Hazard is his surrogate father.

And her own antiwar sentiments, born when she moved to London and along with other teenagers marched in Trafalgar Square in ban-the-bomb movements, found expression in Samantha. Despite the ceremony and pageantry of a military unit like the Old Guard, she says, "It's pretty obvious what it stands for . . . it's an advertisement for the war machine. I've always abhorred war . . . But I don't think I'm going to be the one to stop it. It's been going on for some time now, and it would seem to be the nature of man. So is it disgusting to watch men parading with guns? I don't know the answer to that."

This ambivalence was essential to Samantha's character: she hated war and yet fell in love with a soldier. (At least one critic found this relationship totally unbelievable; others thought it stretched credibility.) Anjelica, asked about the apparent difficulty, said she could never have played the role if she did not believe an antiwar activist like Samantha could really be attracted to Sergeant Hazard. "The heart does not always follow the head, and sometimes unusual things happen in what you find attractive." She recalled the first days of the movie, when all the men had long hair. Then, that first week, all their hair was shaved off. "My reaction was not the horrified reaction I might have had on the first day of meeting them," she said. "I found it extremely attractive. I haven't found it [shaved heads] attractive before or since, but for the time we were shooting, it looked great to me to see the backs of their heads. And," she admitted, "there is something about men in uniform . . ."

There was also something about Arlington National Cemetery itself that Anjelica found very moving. "It makes your hair stand on end," she said, adding that her first sight of it was "overwhelming." The terrible waste of all those lives impressed her: against the background of a real "garden of stone," Anjelica found a way to work out some of her own feelings of loss.

A real loss that occurred very early in the filming affected all of the production crew throughout the rest of their work. Francis Coppola's son, who was a production assistant, was killed in a freak boating accident on Chesapeake Bay. Anjelica remembered feeling futile, having a sense of "What are we doing here? Why are we making movies when things like this happen in real life?"

The death of Coppola's son made her think of

her own mother's death. "A light goes out," she said. "Quite literally, a light goes out and you wonder what you're doing here."

Of course they kept on and finished the film. As Huston said, "Grief is part of life. I think from grief springs the most beautiful things, the purest emotions, the closest affiliations. It's not just a downer—if that's your approach to life, you deny yourself a lot."

That statement shows how far Anjelica Huston had come from the first hard months after her mother's death—months that stretched into years of fear and self-doubt. When Anjelica talks about Jack Nicholson, it becomes clear that meeting him had a great deal to do with the eventual healing that took place, and that their relationship has helped Anjelica achieve the assured maturity behind her acting in roles like Samantha Davis.

Many observers see a resemblance between John Huston and Jack Nicholson, implying that Anjelica was attracted to Jack in the first place because of this "father" image. When asked outright if there is not something of John Huston in Jack Nicholson, Anjelica doesn't duck the question. She has never been attracted to weak men, she says. And there probably is some element of her father in Jack. The two are alike in that neither is ever boring, Anjelica believes. And most important of all—Jack has a great sense of humor. That, she says, may be the most attractive thing about Jack.

She also sees something of her mother in Nicholson. "There's a certain kind of square-earthed presence about Jack that reminds me of my mother," Anjelica told an interviewer. Still, the fact that Jack has facets of both her father's and her mother's personality hasn't made Anjelica "make daughterlike concessions . . . I think we deal pretty straight."

That straight dealing extended to Jack's roaming in the early years of their relationship. Enrica Huston couldn't accept John's womanizing; her daughter has been able to take Nicholson's in stride.

She thinks the Playboy ethic affects a lot of men. "It's hard for men to allow themselves the ease of feeling that they don't have to be the dominant male. Or they don't have to be the seeker, the tryer, the adventurer." She thinks, too, that since Jack didn't grow up thinking he was attractive, he's had to compensate for that by proving to himself—and to others—just how attractive he is. But there's no question that Nicholson is more settled now than when he and Anjelica first began their relationship. Anjelica sees the change. "Jack . . . is less inclined to be that sort of man now than he was when I first met him. He's well-adjusted . . . [and] so intelligent that, ultimately, he would come to a basic and good understanding of the importance of women in the world . . ."

Thirteen years after the Huston-Nicholson affair began, there was not the slightest vestige of Anjelica the Moan, as Nicholson used to call her. In the summer of 1986, with two quite different movie roles behind her, and one Academy Award, Anjelica Huston at thirty-five years of age had come into her own.

CHAPTER 9

ANJELICA'S next role would be the most poignant of all, for many reasons. First of all—although no one could have known it at the time—*The Dead* would be the last film John Huston directed. And secondly, the subject matter of the film would take Anjelica, her brother Tony, and their father on an emotional journey into the past. *The Dead* is taken from a short story by James Joyce. It is set in Ireland. Tony wrote the script, John Huston directed it—and Anjelica stars as Gretta Conroy, like herself a Galway girl.

The film finished production in the spring of 1987; John Huston would live until late August of

that year. And although he did begin work on another movie—*Mr. North*, directed by his son
Danny—he would become too ill to continue in
the role. Robert Mitchum would step into the
breach. Whether John Huston had any intimation
that he would never direct another movie can't be
known. (He directed *The Dead* in a wheelchair and
had a portable oxygen tank.) But certainly he
could have chosen no better valedictory than a
film set in his beloved Ireland, based on a story by
James Joyce, one of the writers Huston always
credited with having made him aware of the possibilities of art.

Selecting "The Dead," the final story in James
Joyce's collection *The Dubliners*, to film took Huston back to his own creative roots, when, in 1929,
while he had not yet decided whether to be a
painter, a boxer, or a writer, his mother gave him
a copy of Joyce's *Ulysses*. John and his first wife,
Dorothy, took turns reading the book to each other
on their honeymoon. The book, banned in the
United States and literally smuggled in by Rhea
Huston, made "doors fall open," Huston said. How
fitting, then, that another Joyce work would help
that final door close. . . .

The Dead takes place at an annual holiday
party given each winter by two elderly sisters for
their family and friends. The film begins quietly as
a variety of guests arrive at the home Julia and
Kate Morkan share with their niece, Mary Jane.
Initially none of the guests seem more important
than the others. The audience is introduced to
Freddy Malins, an alcoholic played by Irish actor

Donal Donnelly; to his anxious mother; and to Mr. Brown, a Protestant whose gentle skepticism is a counterpoint to Aunt Kate, played by Helena Carroll, and Aunt Julia, played by Cathleen Delany, who stick to traditional Catholic ways.

Various young ladies who study music with Mary Jane (Ingrid Craigie) join the party, as well as Bartell D'Arcy (Frank Patterson), whose tenor voice will later delight the gathering. All of the Irish types appear to be here, including a politically minded young woman, who will later turn a casual comment by another guest into an open conflict.

And then the Conroys arrive. The camera pays more attention to Gabriel and Gretta from their first moment in the house, and something about them—Gabriel's literary pretensions, his attempts to assume a European sophistication—tells the audience that here is a capsule ready to be opened, a bubble ready to be burst.

By the time Gabriel, a literary journalist by profession, makes his speech at the end of the meal preparatory to leading a toast to the three hostesses, the inevitability of some sort of private or public explosion seems assured. The very care with which Gabriel chooses his literary quotations in order that his aunts may not be embarrassed by the greater knowledge of their favorite nephew speaks volumes. And as he touches on the traditions of Irish hospitality that are already in danger of being lost, as he reminds the group of other such parties here in his aunts' house, it becomes even clearer that this event, so long anticipated, so pleasantly taking place, is already on its way to becoming a memory. It has no more permanence than does any other experience in life.

That realization, as yet not fully articulated, is followed by the revelation that makes Gabriel Conroy look back at, and reassess, his entire life. He and Gretta leave the party, driving to the hotel where they will spend the night before returning to their own home in the morning. Gretta's mood, festive at the beginning of the evening, has grown increasingly pensive and sad. Finally she tells Gabriel that a song the tenor sang at his aunts' party has stirred up old memories, and that she is thinking of a young man with whom she had a brief, innocent romance before he died at the age of seventeen. She had last seen him the night before she left for boarding school: although he was ill, he got out of bed and came to serenade her, standing in the cold outside her window, singing the song the tenor sang that night.

This confession of something so important to his wife, and yet unknown to him for all the years of his marriage, at first arouses Gabriel's jealousy before it compels him to examine his own life, and to recognize its failings and emptiness. It is left to the viewer to decide whether Gabriel's self-recognition is negative, in that he sees himself and indeed everyone gathered at his aunts' house that evening as already spiritually dead, or whether the self-recognition is positive in that Gabriel gains a new perspective on his own life from seeing its continuity with the dead, and with the past that he himself thought forgotten.

Anjelica believes that her character, Gretta, has already come to terms with the transience of life, and with the fact that it is, in one sense, a series of losses. Gretta loves Gabriel and her children very much—she has been married to Gabriel a long time, she is a kind person, a nice woman. "I don't think the dead boy, Michael Furey, was meant to represent her one true love," Anjelica said. Commenting that Gretta has "held the memory of the boy inside of her for so long" that it must come out, Anjelica recognizes the truth of Gretta's line, "I'll never be that girl again."

This, Anjelica affirms, is true for everyone. Once our hearts have been broken, they can be broken again—but not in quite the same way as that first time. Nor will death ever shock us again as much as it does the first time it strikes us.

Not much older than Gretta is in the film when Anjelica experienced her first terrible loss, the death of her mother, she was able to draw on that experience to give the right depth to Gretta's character. And Anjelica is also certain that Gretta and Gabriel will have a more intimate relationship now that she has told him of this long-ago first love. "They will look and speak differently to each other hereafter," she said.

The Dead proved the perfect story for what would be the last film John Huston directed. It took him and the two children who shared the glorious life at St. Clerans with him full circle, allowing them to make a love-offering to the land where they spent so many happy years. It gave him an opportunity to confirm his legacy to these two children: Tony with the screenplay, and Anjelica with yet another challenging role. Nor did he go easy on himself by selecting the Joyce story to film.

The mode of the story, its quiet unfolding, tested even John Huston's talents to the utmost. As the film's editor, Roberto Silvi, said, "It's very difficult to cut . . . Nothing is easier to edit than action, but dialogue of this complexity is very tricky."

The reunion of Anjelica and Tony Huston with their father was perhaps the happiest effect of the entire endeavor. Separately, both Anjelica and Tony had worked with their father—Anjelica on *Prizzi's Honor* and Tony on another screenplay completed prior to work on *The Dead*. But this was the first time since the days at St. Clerans that the three could spend time together in any significant way.

"This was truly a reuniting of the family," Tony Huston said. "But this time in creative terms." Commenting on how fortunate both he and his sister were to have been involved in what would be their father's last film, Tony said that "in the case of this project, his timing was unbelievable."

As Anjelica said, "When I speak of Galway in the movie, that's something that's right there for me. It wasn't as though I weren't equipped by all sorts of fortune and circumstances to play this role." Tony, too, drew on memories of growing up in Ireland to give the film the authenticity and truth his father required. He could, he felt, "go for the truth of the subject," avoiding the clichés so often used to convey the Irish temperament, and the stereotypes that have become familiar characters on the screen.

Adding to the authenticity of the film was the cast. Anjelica was the only member not Irish-born—and she of course was Irish-bred and still carries a passport issued by her adopted land. The other actors and actresses came from Dublin's Abbey and Gate theaters, and included some of Ireland's leading players. Anjelica found being with those actors for eight weeks "like living in Ireland again." Actually she had not known many Irish people when she lived at St. Clerans as a child. Through working on *The Dead* she came to know the "searing humanity" of the Irish, and to be "staggered at how good they were." In drawing on her own past to make Gretta real, Anjelica could come to terms with the losses that had occurred during the Irish period of her life and hold on to the valuable creative and personal legacy instead.

She was able to prove, too, that her tour-de-force performance in *Prizzi's Honor* was no fluke. The magnitude of her skill and talent became even clearer during the filming of *The Dead*: her brother Tony called her performance in her last scene in *The Dead* her "most powerful accomplishment." Roberto Silvi compared Anjelica to Anna Magnani, and John Huston declared that his daughter had become mature and self-confident with this film.

Tony Huston said that in the last months before his father's death, he spent an extraordinary amount of time with Tony, Anjelica, and Danny, as though he wanted to make sure that each fully understood and could handle the creative legacy he was leaving them. Once *The Dead* was completed, in the spring of 1987, John and Tony began work right away on another screenplay, *Revenge*, and John planned to play the lead in the film *Mr. North*, based on the novel *Theophilus North* by Thornton Wilder, and directed by Danny.

It was as though, Tony said, his father wanted to do something about the first thing on his list of things he would do over if he could. That sentence, written on the last page of Huston's autobiography, *An Open Book*, said, very simply: "I would spend more time with my children." "It's like Dad to do something about those things he could," Tony said.

That time with his children must have made it easier for John Huston to go, when the time came. All the wounds had healed, all the chasms had been crossed. Huston's recognition of his daughter as a powerful actress, and the time they spent together during the filming, must have done much to make up for the gaps in their relationship in earlier times. Anjelica found her father much more emotionally accessible in those last few years together, and easier to get along with than he had been in years gone by.

Although Tony commented that his father looked ten years younger since he began work on *The Dead*, adding that "work and yet more work is what keeps Dad going," the truth of the matter was that John Huston's health had been precarious for years. Although he had survived heart problems dating from a diagnosed heart murmur when he was twelve, and culminating in open-heart vascular surgery for an aneurysm in an aorta in 1977—the very condition that had killed his father—the emphysema that had been his nemesis for decades kept him literally tied to an oxygen tank during the filming of *The Dead*. His illness also kept the production tied to California. Huston, who in his prime made movies on location in places like the Belgian Congo and French Equatorial Africa without giving harsh Nature an inch, couldn't travel to civilized Dublin where the story was set, but had to construct the interior of the turn-of-the-century Irish parlor in a warehouse in Valencia.

Huston's health also limited work days to six hours, an impossibly short time given the complexity of the task of bringing the Joyce story to life on film. But the filming stayed on schedule, and the first cut of the movie was finished four weeks after the last day of production.

It was, Anjelica said, "extremely painful to watch someone whose mind was so vital laid low by bodily matters." She coped with her father's illness from day to day. And, as she commented, everyone around John Huston had always taken care of him. "All the time I was growing up, I couldn't imagine him buying even a tube of toothpaste for himself," she said. "Taking care of him was a full-time job even before he was sick." But she noticed a definite difference in her father's disposition. "Somewhere along the line he's become more human, more accessible. Now he is gentler and more emotionally generous than he ever was."

Answered her father, overhearing that comment—"Only because I treat her as an actress rather than a daughter."

Although Huston refused any sympathy and did not indulge in self-pity, his daughter felt anger for him. "When I think of how many of us abuse our health and how he fought to survive, I become angry. I wish above all things that he could have had his full health on a daily basis."

Others on the set found it painful to watch John Huston's struggles, too. Many of the crew had worked with him before: like Francis Coppola, Huston liked to surround himself with familiar faces, to create, as Anjelica said, "that family thing where you're all working together and there's such excitement. You feel the man has an idea and knows where he's going."

Not that Huston kept such a tight creative rein on his actors that they felt they had to ask him before they tried something. But, said his daughter, "you can speak to him and he'll give you a key, perhaps the voice of the picture . . . some little secret . . . It's the gift, and the vision, and the power. It makes you want to please him more than anything in the world, and when you do, you feel great."

And Tony compared the way he felt when his father approved his writing with the way he felt as a little boy when he showed Huston one of the drawings done on that great Florentine bed.

Apparently the desire to please Huston was of equal importance to the Irish actors, who held him in great awe. None of them had worked with Huston before, nor were they familiar with Huston's directing technique, which he himself summed up as "less is more." In Huston's view, directors who do a take over and over again, each time correcting one thing they don't like only to catch a new flaw, don't realize that "the first time they got it was as good as they were ever going to get it, and all those other takes were complications they made for themselves."

Tony and Anjelica Huston saw this "less is more" approach work over and over again during the filming of *The Dead*. From the first rehearsal Huston used his "hands off" technique. Tony read the descriptive passages in the script while the actors read their lines. Huston said nothing during that run-through, simply thanking them at the end. He actually closed his eyes while they went through the script a second time. The result of this "benign neglect," according to Tony, was that "the more inanimate he appeared, the more the ensemble scenes came alive with singing and clapping" as the actors lost the last vestiges of self-consciousness and settled down to real work.

Even when Huston did offer suggestions, they were said with the same succinctness with which he gave Katharine Hepburn the now-famous instruction on how to play Rosie Sayer in *The African Queen*. "Think of Eleanor Roosevelt," he'd told Hepburn. "Think of her smile." In *The Dead*, when the actor playing Freddy Malins, the alcoholic whom everyone at the party watches anxiously to make sure he does not take too much to drink, seemed to be overplaying his role, Huston told him that Freddy was on hooch, not cocaine.

In another instance, Cathleen Delany, one of the spinster aunts, seemed to have difficulty getting the exact tone for her role. Asking that she be brought to him, Huston told her to think of herself as a little bird. And to Tony he added, "Tell her she's a wren!"

Coupled with this ability to put subtle directions into comprehensible words was John Huston's courtesy toward the actors and actresses with whom he worked. Anjelica of course had seen this when she worked in *Prizzi's Honor*: Huston's method was to take a person aside, or to whisper the advice so no one else could hear it. Said Tony, "I came to see his technique as a sequence of hushed, private conversations."

This low-key approach was particularly well-suited to *The Dead*, a film of which John Huston wryly observed that there was not one automobile chase in the entire thing. There is not a great deal of "action" as moviegoers are accustomed to seeing it in *The Dead*. There is instead a portrayal of the dramatic value of life itself, the gradual unfolding of the thoughts, feelings, and innermost secrets of the guests at the party.

The dramatic possibilities of the story lie in the recognition by each viewer that it is within the confines of intimate gatherings like the one on film that the most explosive confrontations can occur. Unprotected by unfamiliarity, with the weaknesses and flaws of each known to most of the others, and with only courtesy and civility as a defense, the guests at such family parties may well expose themselves to interior violence of the most painful and revealing kind.

And indeed, in the long first section of the film, the party itself, a world where civility and courtesy form the front line against self-knowledge and acceptance of the human condition, is lovingly and carefully drawn. There is dancing, there is singing, there is conversation about the sort of topics that seem both interesting and "safe."

And then, as so often happens when families gather, one small incident—in this case, a tenor's choice of a song—triggers the memories that lie beneath the surface and yet are never really completely gone. What memories must have come into the conscious minds of all three Hustons, as they lived once again at St. Clerans, celebrated once again the splendid Christmases, the bountiful feasts! But now the children were all grown-up, and Huston had a wisdom that he had not had in those years when, as Anjelica said, she and Tony were "half-orphaned" by a father who was so rarely there. And so there were no tears shed during the making of *The Dead*—not on the set, at any rate. Instead a spirit of joy and closeness permeated the entire film. In the truest sense the Huston family had come home.

From this closeness came a freedom to have fun. Tony and John teamed up to play a joke on Anjelica, telling her that they had decided to change the story line. Gretta's past love would be a young girl instead of a boy, they said. "You have never seen such a look of consternation" when they told that tale to Anjelica, Tony remembered. "I wish I'd been able to hold a straight face longer," he said. His expression tipped Anjelica off—while Tony "cracked up," she "grabbed a broom and pretended to sweep us both off the set."

The whole crew—carpenters, grips, all of them—watched the movie's rushes every night. Then John Huston went back to his motel—he had come to Valencia from his home in Puerto Vallarta—to exercise his lungs by forcing them against the pressure of a machine. Maricela Hernandez, Allegra's nurse, waited for him there. That friendship had gone on for ten years, longer than any of Huston's marriages. After a supper of cottage cheese and grapefruit, Huston would read or watch the news on television or perhaps play backgammon with Tony. "Two swigs of a healthy intoxicant" before bed—such a routine was hardly in the pattern of Huston's robust life.

But if Huston had to come to such a semi-invalid state, certainly his luck held out. His daughter attended him with a filial devotion that he himself said was "very comforting." Observers on the set noticed how close the two had become. One recalled watching Huston focus on the monitor as Anjelica finished a scene. "Very good," he said. She came over to him, whispered something in his ear, began to rub his back. And besides the love and care of his children, the work itself kept him going.

"Left to their own devices, his doctors would advise he never leave the hospital," Anjelica said. "But he's no fool. He knows all this keeps him going. It's when he's idle and bored that we have to rush him into intensive care."

John Huston would be dead himself before the film opened in New York on December 17, 1987. But the reviews would have made him smile. Despite the fact that *The Dead* is a complete departure from the kind of movies John Huston always made, it was an artistic and personal triumph.

Vincent Canby wrote: "That Huston should have dared search for the story's cinema life is astonishing. That he should have found it with such seeming ease is the mark of a master." Of Anjelica, Canby says, "Miss Huston is splendid . . . Direction and performance are seamless . . ." *People* magazine critic Peter Travers said, *"The Dead*, alive with John Huston's passion for his craft and those he loved, is a movie masterwork." Other critics called it "absolutely delightful and endearing." And in Dublin, where it opened the Dublin Film Festival early in December 1987, it was received with affection and acclaim.

Said Donal Donnelly, referring to the propensity of filmmakers to show the Irish as fey people with no real relationship to a workaday world, "John and Tony Huston have changed all that. They're showing the Irish as they are, not kowtowing to any preconceived notion of others."

John Huston would have liked that comment.

He had spent some of the happiest times of his life in Ireland, and the lifestyle there more nearly approximated life as he believed it should be lived than that he had anywhere else.

One of the last lines of *The Dead* is: "Better pass boldly into that other world, in the full glory of some passion, than fade and wither dismally with age." Commented John Huston—"That says it."

Although he lived some months past the completion of *The Dead*, the film still provided John Huston with an opportunity to "pass boldly into that other world," and it gave Anjelica an opportunity to prove to her father before he died that she could meet the demands of his personal and artistic legacy with her own creative maturity and control.

And *The Dead* proved, once and for all, that the third generation of the Huston cinematic dynasty has all the charisma, intelligence, fascination, vision, and ability of the two that have gone before. Tony came into his own as a scriptwriter, Anjelica came into her own as a leading lady of both substance and style, a woman who no longer lived in the shadow of the famous man who was her father or the famous man who was her lover, but who emerged into the light, a woman firmly in charge of every aspect of her life.

CHAPTER 10

MR. North was to be another Huston family endeavor. John would play the title role, Anjelica would co-star, Danny would direct. John took a house in Newport, Rhode Island, where the film was to be made. It would be the second time Danny directed his father: John had been in a one-hour short subject for the BBC the previous year. Titled "Mr. Corbett's Ghost," it was, Danny said, "a piece of cake" to direct. He and his father agreed on everything, Danny said, the only problem being that the elder Huston sometimes forgot who was the director and called out "Cut!" at the end of a scene.

But Huston's emphysema hospitalized him soon after he arrived in the East. Knowing how fragile his health was, John had already arranged for Robert Mitchum to take over his role in the event that he became ill. Later Mitchum regaled an audience at a memorial tribute at the Directors Guild in Los Angeles with the tale of his first visit to Huston in the hospital.

Huston seemed in both good health and good spirits, Mitchum said. "John, you suckered me," he told Huston.

"Biggest hoax I ever pulled off, kid," Huston said.

Mitchum thought John looked as if he hadn't been getting enough to eat, and he decided to prove it. He went out to the nurses' station and brought back a very pretty young nurse, and thereupon talked her into slowly raising her skirts.

Just as the hem reached a critical point, Huston held up his hand. "Stop," he said. "You're right, kid. I'm not getting enough to eat."

Hospitalized at the Charlton Memorial Hospital in Fall River, Massachusetts, for twenty-two days, Huston was released on August 19. He returned to the Newport home. Though he had recovered from the pneumonia that had hospitalized him, he still battled emphysema: everyone must have known he could not last much longer. Not only Anjelica, Tony, and Danny were with Huston, but Maricela Hernandez as well. The four watched Huston fight—but by Friday, August 28, he had reached the end of his strength. He had asked that his children not see him in his last hours. Maricela kept that last vigil, and it was she who told the others his last words. He went out fighting, in the mode of an officer defending a fort, harking back to his days with the Mexican cavalry when he was but twenty years old.

Turning to Maricela, John demanded, "How many express rifles do we have?"

"Thirty, John," she told him.

"How 'bout ammunition, baby?" John asked.

"Oh, we got plenty of ammunition," Maricela said.

John reached out and took Maricela's hand, raising it in the air like a prize fighter claiming victory. "Then give 'em hell!" he said.

Anyone knowing John Huston would realize the appropriateness of that last take.

Anjelica believes her father knew he would die that day. "I think he knew pretty well where he was going," she told mourners at a Directors Guild memorial tribute on September 15. "Or maybe not where he was going, but that he was going."

John Huston's ideas about an afterlife are not known. Anjelica says she has many thoughts. She thinks of what John Lennon told his son, that if there were life after death, he would float a white feather across a room so that his son would know his father still lived. She said that she still looks sometimes for her mother to float a white feather across the room—this in an interview a year or so before her father's death.

Still, she does fantasize that she might be re-incarnated on another planet, and the whole question of reincarnation intrigues her. "I am a searcher," she says. "I believe in karma and things coming back to you as you give them out, and I think if the nuns taught me anything, it was that sense of doing to others as you would have them do unto you, because what goes out comes back."

Again, Anjelica isn't sure about reincarnation. Talking to friend Joan Buck, she said that she wished "a little light could be shed on this, because it would be comforting to know that one had been here before." Still, Anjelica doesn't speculate on who she might have been in a previous life—though since she responded to Joan's statement that she might have been a jester at the court of Philip II of Spain by saying it was such a relief that Joan didn't say she had been Cleopatra or Henry VIII, it is safe to assume she would not pretend to have been a historic figure.

"Rather than go from one life to another life, I think I live a lot of lives at the same time," she finally decided—and that is probably fairly close to what her father would have said, had he ever spoken on the subject.

The one short section of John Huston's autobiography that deals with religion closes with these words: "The truth is that I don't profess any beliefs in an orthodox sense. It seems to me that the mystery of life is too great, too wide, too deep, to do more than wonder at. Anything further would be, as far as I am concerned, an impertinence."

The friends gathered at the Directors Guild tribute knew the measure of the man they came to mourn. Among them were Robert Mitchum, Lauren Bacall, Ray Stark, Warren Beatty, Elliot Gould, Billy Wilder—and Jack Nicholson, who, with director Richard Brooks, served as moderator. Nicholson could not hold back his tears as he spoke words that, he told the crowd, he had found by rolling a Chinese fortune-telling device. Nicholson listed those things Huston hated most. "Any dish that contained chicken, mawkish popular songs, people who strain too hard for social correctness—and women who get drunk."

In the days following John Huston's death, newspapers across the country published tributes to him, recaps of his life and career, interviews with people who had known him.

Burt Lancaster, who worked with Huston in *The Unforgiven*, called Huston an "extraordinary man and an extraordinary director." Frank Sinatra considered Huston a giant, while Burgess Meredith, who co-starred with Huston in *The Cardinal*, the first movie in which Huston had a serious role, believed that Huston's secret was that "He was a fearless liver, that is, he lived fearlessly."

And Robert Loggia, a co-star in *Prizzi's Honor*, spoke for all those who worked with Huston over his long career and fell under his unique spell when he said that Huston "worked with a cast like a master conducting a symphony." Speaking of the love and loyalty which Huston generated in those he worked with, Loggia described his grief at Huston's death by saying that he "had the same devastating feeling when my father died."

As would be expected when a man like John Huston was the subject, not everything written about him was fulsome praise. Andrew Sarris, writing in the *Village Voice* a few weeks after Huston's death, said, "John Huston lived and worked long enough to confound even his most determined detractors. This reviewer was among those who had once complained that Huston's life was his art, but in the end, the stirring, life-affirming image of a grizzled prospector of a director with his own oxygen tank near at hand on the set suggested that his art had become his life." And although Sarris, in agreement with others who noted the spottiness of Huston's work—the films of the Fifties and Sixties are generally considered works made during a "dry spell" of creativity—didn't give full marks to Huston's total body of work, he also agreed with other critics that films like *The Treasure of the Sierra Madre, The Maltese Falcon, The Asphalt Jungle, Fat City, The Man Who Would Be King*, as well as *Prizzi's Honor* and a number of other lesser-known films, earned John Huston a high place in the annals of moviemaking.

Others commented on Huston's ability to pick himself up off the canvas, figuratively speaking. Wrote Mike Clark in *USA Today*, "The eighty-one-year-old workhorse . . . directed for almost five decades, long enough to go from overnight success to longtime has-been, to comeback filmmaker of the decade."

Anjelica, Tony, and Danny Huston were bombarded on all sides by discussions about their father and his work, all of this taking place at the same time they were coming to terms with the fact that he was dead, and that they were the Hustons who must carry on the tradition begun by their grandfather Walter and maintained so brilliantly by their father.

Jack Nicholson, who had once said that when Huston died he would cry for the rest of his life, stayed even closer to Anjelica in the days following her father's death. He had lost someone very important to him, too, and in their mutual mourning a new dimension in their relationship formed.

In fact, Nicholson planned to accompany Anjelica to the Santa Fe Film Festival, scheduled for September 16 to 20. Huston was to be honored at that festival: although he had been making movies for almost fifty years, this was the first time a festival centered around his work.

"If only I were seventy-five again and didn't have to breathe air out of a tank, I would surely be there for this most complete retrospective ever given to a filmmaker in America," Huston wrote the festival planners. His death turned the festival into a memorial tribute to the man the chairman of the organizing committee, John Silver, called the director who "made some of the most significant movies with some of the most significant actors."

Not only Anjelica, Tony, and Danny were to attend the festival, but also Lauren Bacall, E. G. Marshall, Zsa Zsa Gabor, Jacqueline Bisset, and Brian Keith. At the last minute Anjelica did not go to Santa Fe for the festival. Her brothers told the press that she had gone to New York to rehearse for *Tamara,* which was to open on October 12 in the Seventh Regiment Armory. (By October 12, Anjelica, who had been signed for a three-month run, was replaced by Marilyn Lighthouse, with no reason given publicly for the replacement.)

Perhaps one reason Anjelica did not go to Santa Fe was a desire to avoid all the questions about her father, and her relationship with him. Both brothers were interviewed extensively, and both showed, in their comments, a somewhat easier history with their father than the one Anjelica had.

Both Tony and Danny saw the last two years of their father's life as an intense effort by John Huston to give his three children the knowledge they needed to succeed in the family business of filmmaking. "It was almost like shift work," Tony said, talking about his father's collaborative efforts with all three children those last months of his life. The three represent John Huston's varied talents: Tony, thirty-eight, has the writing ability, Anjelica, thirty-seven, is the actress—and Danny, twenty-six, has the director's eye.

"We will form a great mafioso strength within the film industry because we all work in different departments," Danny said. He believed that his father wanted the three to carry on his film work— "It seemed to be what he wanted."

Tony agreed that Huston did more than just encourage his children to enter the movie industry. "Dad was somebody who was very, very good at making things happen. In the very best sense of the word, he was manipulative. Dad was able to incorporate us into projects and to introduce us to people who could help us."

This triumvirate is especially rewarding for three adults who, as children, hardly knew each other well enough to have the rivalries and squabbling so typical of siblings. Tony and Anjelica saw more of each other, since they both lived at St. Clerans. But when Ricki left Huston and moved to London, Tony stayed in Ireland, and Anjelica saw him only at holidays. Danny, who grew up in Italy with his mother, also got to know Tony and sisters Anjelica and Allegra at Christmas and holidays only.

"As much as anyone can be a gypsy family, that's what ours was," Tony said.

Like Anjelica, the sons remember their father as "almost like a pirate figure" when they were children. Danny has an early memory of visiting the set where John was making *The Bible* and being shown all the animals of the ark, and Tony remembers seeing Gregory Peck strapped to the big white rubber whale for *Moby Dick*.

And also like Anjelica, they didn't really miss Huston when they were growing up. His power intimidated them, and he always had so many people around him, so much activity going on, that there was little room for children.

"For most of his life Dad was so vital he didn't have time for anything but the next adventure," Tony said, adding that Huston was not really interested in children. "What he liked was people who had knocked around and had a realistic assessment of the world. His friends were rarely from the film business. They were from wildly diverse fields. He loved characters. And he kind of waited until we turned into characters. Toward the end of his life, he really couldn't have enough of us."

John Huston made the time he spent with his grown children productive, taking each of them in hand and teaching them the rudiments of their craft.

First he worked with Danny in "Mr. Corbett's Ghost." Then, while Huston was in England for that filming, a friend sent him a film script that needed work. Tony, of course, had been writing for years. Now the master took him in tow, beginning what Tony described as an intense collaboration over the last years of Huston's life.

The two would meet: John would show Tony how to organize the important elements of a scene, then send him home to write it. They would meet, discuss the results, and move on to the next scene. "The way you learn is not so much by somebody telling you as by your doing it," Tony said. "And Dad was like a Zen monk who kind of hits you in the back with a stick and you suddenly see what you didn't see beforehand. Something's either right or it isn't right, and you should be able to see it instantly."

Danny had actually had a headstart on this sort of tutoring when he assisted his father with *Under the Volcano* a year or so before he directed him in the television film. According to Danny, the word that best describes John Huston's work is "professionalism." "The Huston credo does not include such terms as 'philosophy,'" Danny said.

Tony, as the eldest, spoke for the entire Huston clan when he summed up the way he felt about those last two years, years filled with personal contact and creative work.

"It has been the greatest joy of my adult life that I was able to collaborate with Dad in a creative way. Because Dad was a creator and you saw him in the very best light when he was engaged in making something." Tony went on to say that since his view of his father is that Huston was "essentially a moral man whose mission was to elevate those around him," the new generation of Hustons must take very good care of the legacy he has passed on.

"Let's try and make good films and not rip off the public for a buck. Let's make films that are art."

Thirty of John Huston's films were shown during the Santa Fe festival, including *Prizzi's Honor*. And if Anjelica, so recently—in terms of the heart—reunited with her father, found it too difficult to expose her private grief to the public eye, no one seeing her steal the movie from Kathleen Turner and making Maerose Prizzi a household word could doubt that as far as Anjelica's portion of the legacy was concerned, it was all art.

CHAPTER 11

SEVERAL projects had been discussed during the last days of filming *The Dead.* Anjelica had thought about making a film of the life of Maria Callas, the fiery opera singer whose personal life was as highly dramatic as any of the great operatic heroines she sang. She has said that she would like to produce films as well as act in them: the Callas story was one option.

But in the spring of 1988, Anjelica accepted the role of Clara in the eight-hour CBS miniseries production of Larry McMurtry's novel *Lonesome Dove.* Set in the late 1800s, *Lonesome Dove* tells the stories of Gus McCrae, an ex–Texas Ranger;

Lorena Wood, a prostitute; and of Clara, the woman Gus loved. Gus leads a cattle drive from Lonesome Dove, Texas: Lorena asks to go with him, as she wants to get away from her life in the small town. On the way, Gus meets up with Clara, whom he has not seen in many years. A gripping novel that stayed on the best-seller list for months, *Lonesome Dove* has all the ingredients to make it a powerful film.

Shooting began in Austin, Texas, in March of 1988, with more filming taking place in Del Rio, Texas, and in New Mexico. Scheduled for broadcast in November 1988, *Lonesome Dove*'s cast includes Robert Duvall as Gus, Tommy Lee Jones as W. F. Call, Ricky Shroeder as Newt, D. B. Sweeney (who also appeared in *Gardens of Stone*) as Dish, Danny Glover as Josh Deets, William Sanderson as Lippy Jones, Robert Urich of "Spenser: For Hire" as Jake, Diane Lane as Lorena, and an eight-year-old Austin girl, Lauren Stanley, as Clara's daughter, Betsy.

And after *Lonesome Dove*? Maybe another comedy. Anjelica told an interviewer after *The Dead* was finished that eventually she would do another movie. "It will be a comedy in the sun," she said. "Crying in the movies is awfully aging."

Whatever the film is, whatever the project, Anjelica has a serenity now that she fought hard to get—and appreciates fully. One of the things she likes best about getting older, she told friend Joan Buck, is that "you're not up for grabs, for criticism anymore. You make a decision, it's made, it's fine, you don't have to go back and rework it. You don't have to apologize."

Joan asked Anjelica if winning the Oscar had anything to do with this assurance. Anjelica replied that she didn't think so. "Maybe the success of *Prizzi's Honor* and the fact that the critics were so nice about it made me feel good about myself as someone working in the public eye. And if I ever had a sense of predestination, that was a time when it seemed fated. It was almost as if I had to wait until I was a certain age before things would come about as I wanted them to."

And she treasures work as something "that doesn't belong to anyone else"—a very powerful feeling for a woman who lived in the shadow of other people's work for so long. Anjelica also finds working with other people on a project rewarding—the blending of individual creativity into the whole, the common work toward a common goal. "Of course, at the end of the film, it's a big, sad party and everyone exchanges addresses," she said. "I used to cry. But when you realize that you're not crying at every wrap party, it's a blessed relief."

Even the worry many actors and actresses have about being typecast doesn't bother Anjelica. "I notice I'm asked to play witches and bad women," she commented, adding that there could hardly be two more different women than Maerose of *Prizzi's Honor* and Gretta of *The Dead*. "You're only typecast because of what people have seen of you," she said, although her agent still gets queries from producers as to whether or not Anjelica really speaks with a Brooklyn accent.

Nor is she concerned with being typecast in life. "I don't have all that great an awareness of how people see me in life," she said. "I don't find myself thinking about it a lot."

She does, however, "get irritated when people counsel me on what I should do with my life, or tell me I should get married, or tell me what I should do. I think people have their role models for happiness, and it helps [them] if others fit into that . . ." Anjelica also thinks that people who go around telling others what they should do with their lives have a critical impulse that is inappropriate—and that annoys her.

Self-assured people often do draw critics, particularly critics who are less sure about themselves, and less able to cope with the inevitability of certain things—the aging process, for one. Anjelica seems to handle even this well. "At a certain point you stop looking at your features, at what you don't like. You start looking at lines and the signs of fatigue rather than at the shape of your mouth."

And she remembers a time when she was very young and she looked down and said to herself, "These are my hands. These are the hands that will always be." And, she said, you see different things happening to your hands as time goes on: at one point she liked the fact that her hands were getting bonier. "The same thing carries us through mentally," she believes. "We recognize what we've always recognized as being ours or close to us, even though those things go through many elemental changes. We follow our life as we do our hands."

She carries this idea of continuity over into

her approach to acting. "An actor definitely has to be in the past as well as in the present; an actor must react to past experiences every minute, every second." Observers who do not act themselves sometimes misinterpret what lies behind a performance that draws on an inner past. One question Anjelica ran into after *Prizzi's Honor* was what relationship there was between Maerose's ability to seek revenge and Anjelica's own response if she were willfully wronged by someone. What it comes down to, she was asked, is—are women potentially crueler than men?

Anjelica did not agree with that idea. She believes that women could be more aware of the consequences of their actions than men are, and that this might stop them from being crueler than men, since cruelty might go hand in hand with the ability *not* to think about consequences. Still, she admitted, women can really hurt people, if they set out to do it. And they may be capable of plotting more than men are—carrying out a plan over the long term.

Considering the things that Anjelica says she hates the most, cruelty to others is totally alien to her personality. She hates public embarrassment, public humiliation. She hates not being able to help someone she loves. She hates the smell of hospitals. And she hates guilt and remorse.

That list makes it pretty clear that those last years of her father's life had a profound impact on her. One of the most important things she learned from him was that while physically John Huston's possibilities became more and more narrow at the end of his life, "his mind expanded and he became more gentle, more loving, more giving, more vulnerable, more creative, more of a father than he ever was before."

Anjelica found this expansion a "fantastic, inspirational thing to witness." It gave her a great deal to think about, a great deal to unravel. "It's such a mystery," she said. "Up until a certain point we have to keep our energy down, subvert it, and when we can't do that anymore for health reasons or whatever, only then can we see life as a glorious thing to be lived, strived for, worked out." She thinks most people take too much for granted, adding that one more thing she really hates is feeling absolutely sick at heart and being surrounded by a beautiful day, a beautiful place. "That's terrible," she said. "What you have to remember is that the great feelings come after the terrible ones."

Her father's death gave a new dimension to her own fear of death. She used to see death as a "black hole that you fall into." Her two close encounters with "the Grim Reaper" took first her mother, and then her father. Before her father died, her fear of falling into that black hole persisted—certainly a reflection of her deep-seated grief and sense of loss when her mother died so young. But after her father's death, "it occurred to me that death might be white light and traveling upward."

Anjelica had always associated this fear of falling into a black hole with flying, and so she has had a longtime fear of flying. Now that she sees death in another light, her fear of flying is less. And even before this revelation she had found that "if there's some sort of crisis going on in my life, when I get onto an airplane I don't think twice about the crisis." The fear was bigger than the crisis, she recalled.

She compared the effect to Los Angeles just before an earthquake. Everyone is complaining about some problem—then the earthquake hits "and you realize the immensity of the universe and how enormous the sky is and how insignificant you are." By the time the earthquake is over, "everyone was giggling in supermarkets. There was a great sense of camaraderie."

At thirty-seven years of age, Anjelica Huston has a maturity that people much older often never attain. Perhaps the difference is that she has learned from everything that has happened to her. And like her father, she very much owns her own life—and allows others the right to own theirs.

That laissez-faire attitude of course is present in her relationship with Jack Nicholson, on whom she places no restraints. Still, she has expressed a desire to have children, saying, "I'd like to have them very much." She had always thought, she said, that she'd like to have a child at age thirty-six. "Thirty-six always occurred to me as the year I would have a child," she commented.

A new Huston baby did not come into the world in 1987—but perhaps there is one waiting in the wings. Nothing could be a more appropriate continuation of the Huston dynasty than a child born of Anjelica, fathered by Jack Nicholson, the man everyone considers "family." As Anjelica said, recalling a time when she was complaining to a friend about Jack, the friend said, "But Anjelica—he's family." And ultimately, Anjelica added, he is.

Although she herself has said that it would probably be very sensible to love someone not in the arts, someone not so prone to the ups and downs that go with artistic territory, she can't imagine herself being with someone not in the arts. "When I think of people who aren't in the arts, I immediately think of politicians for some reason, and I would never want to be with a politician."

And since, despite Nicholson's reputed "wildness," Anjelica sees him in a totally different light, saying that there have been many times when "he was the cooling hand on my brow," and since they seem to have worked out a perfect life, there is no reason for Anjelica to be with anyone else.

Jack has his routine, Anjelica has hers. He likes to stay up late and get up toward noon when he's not working on a film. Business matters take up some time, and then Nicholson exercises. He varies the nature of the exercise, sometimes running in the canyon near his house, sometimes swimming, playing tennis, or working out on his Nautilus machines. He's a big sports fan, especially of the Los Angeles Lakers. "Basketball seasons are like wines," he says, "and every wine is different." He goes to all the home games he can and watches the rest on television. Anjelica sometimes watches the Lakers with him, although she is not the fan he is. Nor does she pay attention to the minutiae that are so important to a real team follower.

Anjelica maintains a bedroom in Jack's house: she'll have dinner with him and then spend the night. And when she is at her own house, the small, pink, Spanish-style house in a West Los Angeles canyon, they spend a lot of time on the phone.

Still, she has made her own life routine, and it is very important to her. "When I sleep at home, I get up slowly and totter around and read the papers and feed the animals." Often Anjelica is wakened by the telephone—she says she is called almost every morning by people who wake up earlier than she does.

She must have inherited her father's love for animals. Although her menagerie doesn't yet require a ranch, as her father's did, still, she has an impressive beginning. Her dog, Minnie, is half Westy and half Lhasa. She has goldfish in a fountain, and an assortment of cats. "I would love to have an elephant," she says, "but they're so hard to transport."

The house itself, rose-colored and tranquil, symbolizes the way Anjelica views her own life— through rose-tinted lenses that bring the good, happy times into sharp focus and use a soft filter on everything else. She has filled the house with memorabilia of her childhood: the Renaissance angel that watched over her while her father was away, the armless teddy bear she still can not throw away. And pictures—drawers full of pictures.

The pictures reflect the dichotomy of Anjelica's early life. There are the ones taken at St. Clerans when she, her mother, and Tony held the fort for the absent master. Those are pictures of an idyllic childhood—riding ponies, playing with pets, or playing with friends. Then there are the pictures of her father—stills shot on location with people like John Wayne or John Steinbeck or Humphrey Bogart.

"God, how I cling to my possessions!" Anjelica says. "It's ridiculous!"

Most people would find it touching. And somehow reassuring that a woman who has had one of Hollywood's top stars as her lover for fifteen years, and who has earned stardom herself—who leads a life filled with glamor and excitement, creativity and approbation—still needs the talismans of childhood to help her feel safe.

But more and more as the adult life around her becomes more and more "real," full of work and prospects of work, the talismans of childhood can lose some of their power, can become mementos of her roots, the roots that held steady and firm until Anjelica was ready to bloom.

Some of the possessions in the house have another meaning. There are eight needlepoint pillows, elaborate designs of crabs and seashells, that Ricki Huston worked during those lonely days in Ireland. Each stitch can serve as a reminder that patience and self-discipline can hold loneliness and despair at bay, and that beauty is a strong weapon against almost every foe.

Anjelica Huston's parents both loved beauty

and were themselves extraordinarily attractive people. Ricki, of course, had the kind of classic beauty that makes people stop and stare. John, while not "leading-man good-looking," had the kind of looks that, combined with the power of his charm, made him stand out in any crowd. He kept this quality even into old age: pictures taken during those last months show a white-haired, white-bearded man, proud nose dominating his face, eyes bright with life.

Anjelica resembles Ricki but is not a classic beauty. She herself remarks that she has one of those faces that if she doesn't keep her chin up, everything collapses and it's a disaster. Taken separately, some of her features are not pretty: her nose is large, her eyes are a little closer together than is normally considered attractive, and their almond shape also makes them different. And her neck is long, making graceful movement imperative. The French have a term for this kind of beauty—*jolie-laide*. It describes a woman who is extremely beautiful one minute—and then, in a twinkling of an eye, looks almost plain. But Anjelica Huston never looks "plain"—like her father, she has an aura, a force, that charges her features and arrests attention. Anyone who saw her in *Prizzi's Honor* saw how Anjelica's individual style of beauty overpowered Kathleen Turner's conventional prettiness. And while such looks will demand certain kinds of roles—so far, those roles have been good for her.

Although she obviously has a great sense of style, she doesn't "put on the full stick" when she's at home, the way Maerose Prizzi did. She wears Levi's jeans and big shirts, often pads around barefooted. Still, she conveys a regal air. One interviewer said of her profile that it "is the kind usually found only on old coins, frescos, or *Vogue* magazine covers."

She smokes a lot, something most people encountering her for the first time notice immediately. She wears distinctive jewelry: lots of gold bracelets at the same time, a pair of earrings with one set with a black pearl, the other with a white pearl. Although she smokes, she doesn't "do drugs." And she thinks that taking drugs is just part of the California life. What it boils down to, she says, is that people who don't have enough to do turn to drugs. She adds that she thinks the whole thing about who does drugs and who doesn't has been "blown out of all proportion." That sounds like something John Huston might say—he had that same cosmic acceptance of what other people did with their lives.

Anjelica has that kind of acceptance about her own life—and about the inevitability of aging. Featured as one of America's Ten Most Beautiful Women in the September 1987 *Harper's Bazaar*, Anjelica was quoted as saying, "When I'm old, I would rather be a blue-haired lady than an attempt at youth regained, cut-up, pulled, and injected." But looking at the elegant woman posed next to the quote, one has no doubt that Anjelica's particular kind of beauty will age well. It's in the bones, and in the special glow that infuses her features with distinction.

Although Anjelica and Jack have been an "item" so long that no other men even try to get close to her—they know she's around. The same month *Harper's Bazaar* named Anjelica one of America's ten most beautiful women, *Esquire* asked the question: WHAT IS IT ABOUT ANJELICA HUSTON? Nine men replied.

Writer Jim Harrison said that she is a "woman of precise and indomitable grace." He said she was "larger than life," comparing that quality to the same quality in John Huston and Jack Nicholson.

Elmore Leonard sees Anjelica as a character in one of his books. She'll "stand waiting with that sleepy look and my guys tripping all over each other to get to her first."

If Leonard saw Anjelica in one of his books, Stanley Bing saw her in a dream, a dream in which he is at Spago (a posh Los Angeles restaurant) with Jack and Anjelica. Jack is called away—and Bing is alone with Anjelica. He thinks of "her rock-hard sinew rippling under a sheath of sleek and burnished flesh. The promise of athletic sex dangles in the air."

Then there are the thoughts of writer Barry Hannah, delivered in his typical writing style. "Big-boned, fetching woman," he begins. He says she looks both trustworthy and vulnerable—which is good. He also sees a "bit of high melancholy about her" and wouldn't be surprised to learn that she writes secret poems and then burns them up. Perhaps Hannah's highest praise is in these words: "She has depth."

The final comment is titled—"And what was said by the one who really knows." Ironically, the speaker quoted is not Jack Nicholson, but John Huston, who probably knew much less about his daughter than the man who had been with her in an intimate relationship for so many years. And what her father said, rather typically, concentrated on him, rather than on his daughter. Recalling a time when he had been in intensive care, Huston said how loyal Anjelica was to him. "I opened my eyes and there was my Anjel. It was most reassuring."

What would Nicholson say if he had agreed to be in that list? Probably much the same as he has said in interviews over the years. He is apparently pleased with the new dimension their relationship has, commenting that with Anjelica so busy now, they naturally don't see as much of each other as before. But, he adds, she is much less dependent on seeing him, much more relaxed about the amount of time they have together.

And at fifty-one, Jack Nicholson may be ready to lead a somewhat more settled life himself. He can pick and choose the roles he wants to do: increasingly, so can Anjelica. In an age where marriage vows often don't last the length of time it takes the wedding silver to tarnish, their relationship has more validity than many that follow those formal "I do"s.

Anjelica's summation of the quality of their relationship says it all. They "share a mutual recognition," she says. While she finds that they don't have time to verbalize everything that goes on between them, she really thinks that what they have is instinctual. "When you meet someone and you look in their eyes, it's like, and if you'll forgive the comparison, looking into the eyes of a good horse or a good dog."

What does Anjelica Huston see when she looks into Jack Nicholson's eyes? "Kindness," she says, "and mutuality that is indescribable." Finally, she says, "There's something that ties you to that person."

In an age of romance, such a feeling, which apparently began the night they first met; would be called "love at first sight." In this age it might be called "fate" or "luck," or just massive physical attraction that evolves into something deeper. Whatever it is, Anjelica and Jack have got it. And what their relationship seems to do is what every great relationship ought to do—it allows each of them to be their best possible selves.

You can't ask for anything better than that.

So what lies ahead for Anjelica Huston?

Looking over the twists and turns her life has taken, it would be presumptuous to even try to predict. But certainly she has proven that she has what it takes to do any number of things. Recalling what she said to friend Joan Buck about living a lot of lives at the same time, and about having a hard time sometimes knowing exactly what all of her characters think at the same time, it might be valid to say that Anjelica seems to have solved that problem. One persona emerged and fleshed out Maerose Prizzi into the outrageous, larger-than-life woman who astonished and delighted the movie critics and audiences as well. Another persona made Samantha Davis in *Gardens of Stone*, the antiwar activist who falls in love with a very traditional military man, believable. Yet another part of Anjelica, reaching back to those golden days at St. Clerans, infused Gretta Conroy in *The Dead* with warmth and feeling.

And still other parts of Anjelica can swing swords wildly in swashbuckling roles like hers in *Ice Pirates*, or fly about on a broom as a witch in *Captain Eo*. Is there no end to her variety?

If she has inherited even one-fourth of her father's genes—probably not.

While many critics divided Huston's films into those that could be considered "art" and those that could not, some more perceptive observers realized that for Huston, the experience of filmmaking was just as engaging—and sometimes more engaging—than the creation of what Huston called "often self-conscious art." "What other occupation could offer such a wild, rushing flow of incident?" he asked once.

Most people could not stand lives filled with "a wild, rushing flow of incident." Most people would agree with the Chinese blessing, "May you live in uninteresting times." And Anjelica, in the way she seeks tranquillity and beauty in her domestic surroundings, apparently agrees with this sentiment at a level that really works in her life.

Ultimately a major difference between John Huston and his actress daughter is this serene core at her center, a core that goes straight back to Enrica Soma Huston's acceptance of the life she entered into when she married the tumultuous, roving genius named John. Where Huston seemed to require constant excitement and stimulation, Anjelica seems to require a more balanced life. Good, creative work; a single relationship with a man who has been like a member of the family as well as her lover since they first met; and a small pink house to cradle it all in.

The phrase "Anjelica Huston comes of age" appeared in many headlines and stories about her in the months following her triumph in *Prizzi's Honor*. Seeing how well she has handled the attention showered upon her, the stellar quality of performances in succeeding roles, a new phrase should supersede that old one.

"The Age of Anjelica" could well describe the exciting years ahead, when, with a sureness and a maturity she herself has earned, Anjelica takes the legacy her father and grandfather passed down to her and enhances it with her own special gifts.

As to whether there will be a son or a daughter waiting to take this treasure from her—that is a question only the future can answer. But should Anjelica Huston and Jack Nicholson have a child—what a legacy that child would be born to! Her beauty, class, and talent combined with Nicholson's audacious charm and awesome skill make an extraordinary genetic blend. And although this child would not have a mystical life in a faraway Irish castle—somehow it seems clear that the life Anjelica would make for that child would have the best of both worlds.

The serene beauty of life with Ricki—the rollicking excitement of life with John.

All kinds of trite sayings come to mind that don't seem to apply when held against Anjelica Huston's life. "You can't go home again" is one. Clearly in *The Dead* she *did* go home again—and only validated the worth of her years in Ireland. "You can't have it both ways"—and yet she does. Not married in the legal sense, more married than many wives in the personal sense. The freedom to pursue her professional career to the utmost—and the security of a long-term relationship to a man who not only loves her but admires her, respects her, and makes her laugh as well.

Neither Walter Huston nor John Huston said much about an afterlife—they were both too busy living this one to the fullest. And yet, if there is any cosmic justice at all, somewhere those two Irishmen's eyes must be smiling.

The kings are dead—long live the queen.

INDEX